CHANGING ATTITUDES TO EDUCATION IN INDIA

K. VENKATA REDDY

ATLANTIC PUBLISHERS AND DISTRIBUTORS

Published by
ATLANTIC PUBLISHERS AND DISTRIBUTORS
B-2, Vishal Enclave, New Delhi-110 027
Phones : 541 3460, 542 9987

Sales Office
4215/1, Ansari Road, Darya Ganj, New Delhi-110 002
Phones : 327 3880, 328 5873, 328 0451
Fax : 91-11-328 5873
e-mail : info@atlanticbooks.com
web : www.atlanticbooks.com

Typeset at
APD Computer Graphics, Delhi

Printed in India at
Mehra Offset Press, Delhi

PREFACE

As education is an organic entity, it changes and grows with the time, responds to the needs of society and adapts itself to the environment. If the education system fails to respond adequately to the emerging challenges of a developing society, the onward march of a nation will stop. Hence, the need for changing our attitudes to education at all levels from Pre-school Education to Higher Education, depending upon the demands of times so as to make it meaningful and relevant to the needs of society.

In India, we have, no doubt, made continuous and consistent efforts to change and modernize our system of education with a view to making it respond to the challenges of a changing society. We have some of the most scholarly documents on our education system by way of reports of Committees and Commissions headed by eminent educationists. Beginning with the report of the University Education Commission (1948) headed by Dr. Radhakrishnan, we have had the report of the Education Commission (1966) headed by Kothari, the National Education Policy (NEP) document of 1986, the Acharya Ramamurthy Committee Report (1990) and the report of the review committee under Janardhan Reddy. These Committees and Commissions have been accepted by the States and the Central Government, but they remain on our shelves, often quoted and scarcely implemented. Especially Higher Education in India represents a system that has successfully resisted any substantial change in the last 50 years. Far removed from meeting the challenges of our times, it is groaning under the weight of accumulated arrears of reforms.

The UNESCO's International Commission for 21st century has called for reforming education by making it a process that is open to all and continuous throughout a person's life time. In a recent report (1996) the Commission lays emphasis on the relationship between education and six subject areas of development — science, economics, citizenship, culture, social cohesion and work. Education in this perspective provides an individual with a set of opportunities through which he equips himself to be an invaluable member of his social group. But, the question is whether education in India is sensitive to these ideals. Does our education take into account the complexity evidenced in our socio-cultural surroundings?

Something apparently seems to have gone wrong with the kind of knowledge, skills and attitudes that we are seeking to impart through the present system of education. Knowledge is more often than not in the forms of knowledge *per se* without any necessary relationship with ecological surroundings. In fact, many academic courses seem to assume that knowledge is autonomous of life patterns and life experiences. Skills learnt through education are often geared towards jobs that have white collar orientation, not always requiring use of manual power. Above all, attitudes formed during the process of education are not always helpful either in social life or in professional life.

In a developing country like India education should aim at facilitating the growth and assimilation of certain concepts, acquisition of usable skills and formation of desired attitudes. The acquired concepts, skills and attitudes have to be further visualized in terms of socio-cultural surroundings of the individual. The need of the hour, therefore, is to make education more productive and responsive to societal needs. Education has to be closely related to the life and aspirations of the people and thereby become a powerful instrument for social, economic and cultural transformation necessary for the realization of our national goals. The emphasis in the education system must be on productivity, strengthening social and national integration and striving to build character by cultivating social, human and moral values. All this calls for a definite change of attitude to the dynamic of education in India.

The present book aims at driving home the changing attitudes to education in India on the eve of the Golden Jubilee celebrations of Independence. Divided into ten distinct chapters, the book deals with the attitudinal changes called for in the realms of children's education, teaching of English in India, modern methods of learning, role of teachers, university education, university library, non-formal education, extension education, bridging the gap between education and life, and education that takes us from a grim today to a grand tomorrow.

I acknowledge my deep sense of gratitude to the educationists whose writings have provided the base for some of the insights that have gone into making of this book. It is hoped that the book would be of considerable interest and use not only to the specialists in the field of education but also to the general public.

K. VENKATA REDDY

CONTENTS

I

CHILDREN'S EDUCATION

1. CHILD AS 'THE FATHER OF THE MAN'

Hoping 'to see into the heart of things', with the help of the child, the idealists, he mystics and the philosophers, in all ages and countries, have made childhood memories the basis of their philosophical quest. Wordsworth, the poet of Man and the high-priest of Nature, is one of the mystics who elevated the child to the highest pedestal. In one of his inspired moments, Wordsworth sings : "Child is the father of the man". What he means by this is that through the recollection and observation of early childhood, we may hope to trace our ancestry — in heaven above or the earth beneath — in its most significant manifestations.

In many ways Wordsworth was an exceptional individual and his childhood had also been exceptional. His memories were more vivid and his thinking more penetrating than those of ordinary mortals. He finds cause for gratitude and praise in the experiences of his childhood, not from admiration for the child's faith in happiness, hope, and liberty :

> But for those questionings,
> Of sense and outward things,
> Fallings from us, vanishings;
> Blank misgivings of a creature
> Moving about in Worlds not realised.

The recollection of his childhood experiences played an important part in Wordsworth's recovery from the spiritual crisis which overtook him after his return from France. These recollections soothed and comforted his soul. In *The Prelude*, he succintly analyses his childhood. Upto the end of his days, he cherishes the memories of his childhood.

He listens to the cuckoo with delight, for it reminds him of his school-days and helps him to "beget that golden time again". Poem after poem records the fascination that children had for him till he bursts out in lyrical raptures in the Sonnet composed on the beach near Calais :

Dear child! dear Girl! that walkest with me here,
If thou appear untouched by solemn thought,
Thy nature is not, therefore, less divine :
Thou lies in Abraham's bosom all the year;
And worship'st at the Temple's inner shrine,
God being with thee when we know it not.

Wordsworth's philosophic attitude towards childhood is best represented by his "Immortality Ode" in which the child becomes,

Mighty prophet, seer blest
On whom those truths do rest
Which we are toiling all our lives to find.

The child has vivid recollection of the life it has already lived in another world, and its mind is not an utter blank :

Not in entire forgetfulness,
And not in utter nakedness,
But trailing clouds of glory do we come,
From God, who is our home.

As the child grows to be a man, the burden of life proves too much for these intimations of immortality, till they fade into the light of common day. But the child, as long as it is child, keeps those celestial visions, and can teach the poet truths which he himself does not know, and has no other means of knowing. Hence, the poet addresses the child as,

Thou best philosopher, who yet dost keep,
Thy heritage, thou eye among the blind,
That, deaf and silent, readst the eternal deep,
Haunted for ever by the eternal mind.

Thus, Wordsworth glorifies children because for him, "they are the very image of God brought up in natural surroundings". It was not by an acquaintance with Platonic philosophy that he arrived at his glorification of childhood, but by looking at nature and life with an open mind. Wordsworth's glorification of the child has, however, been criticised as visionary and mystical, without any basis of justification in fact. But, it should be remembered that Wordsworth was a poet and not a philosopher. Hence, it would be a mistake to regard his attitude as a coherent theory or philosophy, and to accept it or reject it as a whole. He has given us a vision, an "inlet to illuminate emotion", in which different minds can share according to their capacities. His optimism makes of human life a continuous immortal thing without beginning or end, and thus brings healing balm for the soul of a suffering, frustrated humanity.

2. THE IMPORTANCE OF PRE-SCHOOL EDUCATION

Little attention was paid to pre-school education in the pre-Independence era in India though a few nursery and kindergarten schools were started in big cities like Calcutta, Bombay, Delhi and Madras by charitable societies and interested private agencies. Only the children of the elite could enjoy the privileges of this type of education. Despite the strong recommendation made by the Central Advisory Board of Education (1944) to make pre-school education an essential adjunct of the national system of education, no programmes of pre-school education were taken up by the British Government.

Only after Independence the Government of India started taking some interest in pre-school education through the Central Social Welfare Board and the Indian Council for Child Welfare. Various voluntary organisations also espoused the cause of pre-school education.

Nonetheless, pre-school education in India is yet to register rapid growth. According to the report of the Indian Education Commission (1964-66), if 50% children of the age group 2-5 were brought under the purview of pre-school educational programme, the enrolment in 1994-95 would be about 5 millions. Though we have entered the 1990s the expectation of the Commission remains a mirage.

The importance of pre-school education could hardly be exaggerated. It is in the pre-school stage that the foundation of child's education is laid. The research evidence indicates the crucial importance of the first five years of a child's life to his physical, socio-emotional development and the retardation likely to result owing to deprivations in his physical and social environment. Recent psychological studies show that 40% of mental development of a child is completed by the time it reaches the age of four years and 80% when it is eight. Hence, the urgent need to give more and more importance to pre-school education.

The aims and objectives of pre-school education are :

(i) to develop in the child a good physique, adequate muscular co-ordination and basic motor skills;

(ii) to foster in the child good health habits;

(iii) to build up basic skills necessary for personal adjustment;

(iv) to develop desirable social attitudes and manners thereby encouraging healthy group participation;

(v) to make the child sensitive to the rights and privileges of others;

(vi) to develop emotional maturity by guiding the child to express, understand, accept and control his feelings and emotions;

(vii) to encourage aesthetic appreciation;

(viii) to stimulate intellectual curiosity in the child;

(ix) to help the child understand the world in which it lives and to foster new interests through giving opportunities to explore, investigate and experiment;

(x) to encourage independence and creativity by providing the child with sufficient opportunities for self-expression; and

(xi) to develop the child's ability to express his thoughts and feelings in fluent, correct and clear speech.

Though pre-school education is so essential, it is a pity that it reaches today only a fraction of our children, that too mostly those who live in urban areas. It is high time the Government directed its attention to the problem of universalizing pre-school education and took concrete measures to safeguard the educational interest of the children of 2-5 age group, especially in the neglected, rural areas.

3. EDUCATION FOR DRAWING OUT THE BEST IN CHILD

Although Mahatma Gandhi declared as early as in 1939 — "I think Basic Education is my best gift to the country during my life time" — it is a pity, indeed, we have been paying only lip service to the cause of Basic Education. If one type of education is most suitable and, what is more, most needed to a developing country like India it is Basic Education which is essentially work-oriented.

The philosophy behind Basic Education is "an all-round drawing out of the best in child and man, body, mind and spirit". A proper and all-round development of the mind can take place only when it proceeds *pari passu* with the education of the physical and spiritual faculties of the child. Basic Education, therefore, begins by teaching the child a useful handicraft and enabling it to produce something constructive and useful from the moment it begins its training. The core of the concept of Basic Education is that handicrafts to the pupils are to be taught not merely for productive work, but for developing their intellect.

Thus, under Basic Education, education is imparted through a productive and creative activity. The child learns through a purposeful activity which stimulates its learning and makes learning a joyous pursuit. The child quickly learns various things by doing. For example, while digging the earth, the child learns about soils, and while spinning learns counting. In the process the child acquires not the superficial literacy, but the far more important capacity of using hand and intelligence for some constructive purpose.

As Basic Education lays emphasis on manual labour, production and self-sufficiency, it helps students choose vocation easily after completion of their education. So, they will not become parasites on society after their education. Moreover, it teaches dignity of labour which is fundamentally lacking in the educated young men and women at present. Instead of simply waiting for white-collar jobs they will employ themselves in some constructive way or other.

Correlation with craft and environment and co-ordination with other subjects is an important aspect of Basic Education. The handicraft is the pivot around which the teaching of other subjects revolve. So, a natural correlation between craft and other subjects and co-ordination among different subjects is achieved. The child does not learn exclusively either with his mind or body but with both his body and mind. This frees the child from the tyranny of purely academic and theoretical instruction against which its active instincts make a healthy protest. Besides, handicrafts teach the child how to see, think and work in a given situation. This helps him gain self-confidence and manifest his capacities.

So, in Basic Education knowledge is not divorced from action as is the case at present. That practical activity is the best means of instruction in all subjects is beyond dispute. Basic craft provides scope for satisfaction of instincts like curiosity and construction. Furthermore, it helps to develop the spirit of investigation, enquiry, exploration, manipulation and experimentation in the student.

Also, Basic Education caters to the varied talents and interests of children by offering different kinds of work. There is no rigid syllabus. The various activities in the programme afford an educationally varied kind of activity which links the individual with his physical and social environment. Thus, education becomes related to life through craft. In this manner, Basic Education enables the student to adjust himself intelligently and actively to his physical and social environment through his craft work which utilises the resources of the physical for the purpose of the social. This gives rise to an activity curriculum which would transform schools and colleges into "places of work, experimentation and discovery".

Through Basic Education pupils can make contribution to group enterprises and for social good too. Self-governing activities are encouraged. Through active participation in social activities and undertakings the student is made aware of the purposes of education which is to develop an egalitarian society based on social justice, truth, non-violence and co-operation. This link-up between education and social responsibility would not only enrich the content of education but also involve the young in the fascinating adventure of building up a new India.

All these sociological and psychological foundations of Basic Education aim at the development of the 'whole person' which is the need of this century. In the words of the well-known British educationist and thinker, Wilfred Wellock, "In the exercise of all man's powers in purposive social living, Gandhi discovered a unifying principle by which the human person might become a whole man, capable of building integrated families, integrated communities and a peaceful world."

It is, therefore, high time both the Government of India and the State Governments devoted special attention to make our educational system work-oriented at all stages. It is futile to regard Basic Education as a fad of the Mahatma. With the serious problems of mounting educated unemployment and growing student unrest, the orientation of our educational system on the lines suggested by Mahatma Gandhi has now become more and more imperative and compelling.

4. A FRESH LOOK AT CHILDREN'S DISCIPLINE

Time was when the Indian child accepted parental or school order without much question. To obey was automatic. This is no longer so. The questioning spirit that began elsewhere has permeated this country. The student will no longer easily acquiesce in authority at secondary level. He will question, argue and demand certain things.

The Indian child of today, whether at elementary or at secondary level, is apt to ask questions that were not asked before. These questions will have to be answered. He will express opinions with a positiveness that may shock parents and teachers who are likely to suppress them lest children should go beyond their control.

If parents and teachers are sensible, they need have no fear of this potential opposition. For, in the long run, children are as sensible as an adult electorate. They may think and talk nonsense, but they make the right active decisions. And respect for parents and teachers will not waver or fail if they conduct themselves with stability, wisdom and good sense.

The need for growth is evident at every stage of education — primary, secondary and higher. With maturity comes a demand for freedom that no wise educationist can resist. The question for us to consider, however, is not the stage at which freedom should be associated with authority, but the ways in which authority and freedom should abide together so that the product of their combined impact will be a nature creature.

Socrates, whose name dominates the world of education after twenty centuries, was a man who questioned authority with freedom and freedom with authority. This man, cheerfully drinking his cup of hemlock, symbolizes the perfect compromise between the freedom to think and question, and the authority that knows that anarchy and disorder are bad for the human spirit.

If, today, we in India consider the question of discipline with new eyes, it is because we see that the student in the elementary and the secondary schools needs for his development a larger measure of freedom than he has had in the past. Conversely, it needs a different kind of discipline.

It is a truism to say that the only desirable discipline is self-discipline. Self-discipline is not easy to achieve, and if we ask of students in elementary and secondary schools that they should achieve this either quickly or at all, we are asking for the proverbial moon.

The only discipline that comes naturally to children in groups is a discipline exercised by that group. Rounding-off angularities, smoothing rough edges are all part of the business of being at school. This is the kind of incidental discipline that is good for all children and that no child ultimately regrets having had.

There is, in addition, the inevitable discipline of a time-table and a curriculum as well as the discipline implicit in the presence of teachers and a headmistress.

Discipline from the home may complement or conflict with the discipline of the school. Ordinarily, parental discipline should enhance the discipline of the school and be enhanced by it.

From the standpoint of the child's freedom, it is clearly important for parents to think harder than they have done in the past. The adolescent can no longer be treated as an automation who grows automatically upwards from childhood to maturity, without problems, maladjustments and those unanswerable questions that parents and teachers have to cope with. Adolescence must be recognized as a difficult period in which an essentially good and kind child, who will eventually achieve maturity and wisdom, passes through a period of adjustment, unhappiness, weariness, fatigue, discontent, frustration and irritation with the world at large.

These irritations are particularly focused on parents and teachers. If parents and teachers cannot survive this period of questioning, scrutiny, criticism, they are obviously not worth the high prestige that they have inherited from a dead past and the reverence in which they hope to be held in a beckoning future.

5. VOCATIONAL TRAINING FOR CHILDREN'S ALL-ROUND GROWTH

A system of education that can help in turning out young boys and girls for various necessary functions through different types and grades of training, suited to the taste and capacity of each, is what a community requires for its well-being. Unfortunately, our present system of education seems to be entirely unrelated to this central demand. What passes as education is, with very few exceptions, purely an academic affair.

This has to be changed forthwith to make education in our schools meaningful and relevant to the felt needs of society. The primary and upper-primary schools, especially in rural areas, have to make provision for compulsory vocational training. Agriculture being the mainstay of the people in India, scientific agriculture, dairy-farming and agricultural industries should be made compulsory subjects for vocational training.

Furthermore, optional courses for various handicrafts such as weaving, tanning, pottery, masonary, basket-making, toy-making, smithy, carpentry, repair of stoves, watches, cycles, musical instruments and transistors should be open to the pupils. The vocational courses in schools must necessarily be of an elementary nature and graded according to the age, taste and the capacity of the pupil.

High schools should provide for a higher standard of vocational training in improved farming, commerce, banking, insurance, book-keeping and modern industries such as chemical industries and motor mechanics. High schools should be essentially academic, and vocational training is to be a subsidiary part of the curriculum so that students may develop a taste for practical work and also gain skills in some craft or other by the time they leave the school.

Such alliance of education with some sort of vocational training has an educational value of its own. It enhances the bread-winning capacity of the student and, what is more, makes for his all-round growth. Training the eyes, ears as well as the hands of the pupils through interesting and purposeful hand-work, goes not only to develop their will and executive ability but also to help a natural unfoldment of their power of understanding.

Modern educational thought is practically unanimous in commending the idea of educating children through some suitable form of productive work. This method is considered to be the most effective approach to the problem of providing an integral, all-sided education to the student for his all-round growth and overall development of personality.

The introduction of such practical, productive work in education is psychologically desirable because it relieves the children from the tyranny of a purely academic and theoretical instruction. It balances the intellectual and practical elements of experience. The child acquires not the superficial literacy, but the capacity of using hand and intelligence for some constructive purpose.

Socially considered, such a system of education tends to break the existing barriers of prejudice between manual and intellectual workers. Furthermore, it cultivates a true sense of the dignity of labour and of human solidarity among students — an ethical and moral gain of incalculable significance.

From the strictly educational point of view, greater concreteness and reality can be given to the knowledge acquired by children by making some significant craft the basis of education. Knowledge will thus become related to life, and its various aspects will be correlated with one another.

6. CO-CURRICULAR ACTIVITIES FOR CHILDREN'S INDIVIDUAL DEVELOPMENT

Time was when mere teaching in the classroom was supposed to be the aim of all school education. But, there has been a shift in the emphasis of what is meant by the term, 'education'. Education is now defined as a continuous process during which stress is laid on the development of the overall personality of the individual student. And, since an average student spends 75% of his time outside the classroom, it becomes all the more important to pay more attention to this part of life than has been done so far.

It is to cater to the needs and demands of the student's life outside the classroom that co-curricular and cultural activities are designed. They include literary activities like essay writing, elocution, debate, discussion, seminar and quiz, cultural activities like acting, singing, dancing, painting, drawing, claymoulding and collage, physical activities like gardening, games and sports and social activities that are taken up under National Service Scheme (NSS) and NCC.

The purpose of this great variety of creative activity is to facilitate the individual development of children into self-directed, responsible and mature adults. These various constructive and nation-building activities also contribute to the achievement of the general objectives of education, especially those related to the individual development of students. Ultimately these creative activities seek

(a) to complement the academic learning of the classroom;

(b) to encourage children in developing means of better utilisation of their leisure;

(c) to aid in the process of social interaction of children;

(d) to assist children in developing better values and higher standards of personal behaviour;

(e) to develop leadership qualities in children;

(f) to promote the social, intellectual and cultural development of children;

(g) to inculcate democratic traditions among the young and to prepare them for self-help; and

(h) to develop a sense of social service and national consciousness among the young students.

All the young students should, therefore, seize each and every opportunity of participating in co-curricular activities as well as in cultural programmes enthusiastically, thereby exploiting their innate capacities and latent potentialities. Some of the children may have to overcome their inhibitions like stage-fear and participate in elocution and debating competitions. Through constant participation they can achieve wonders. Let us remember that participation in co-curricular activities is more important than getting a prize. Nothing will give children more pleasure than a sense of self-fulfilment which would go a long way in fostering their individual development, the richest possession of the young world, indeed !

7. TOWARDS DESCHOOLING OF CHILDREN'S EDUCATION

For generations, we have simply assumed that the proper place for education to occur is in a school. It is now gradually realised that this age-old assumption is ill-founded. The current thinking on the part of modern educationists is in terms of getting education deschooled to the extent possible with a view to making it more functional and meaningful.

The basic background of the present school system almost parallels that of the factory. Children who enter the school quickly find themselves part of a standard and basically unvarying organisational structure — a teacher-led class. As they move, grade by grade, to the higher levels, they remain in this same fixed organisational frame. They gain no experience with other forms of organisation. They get no training for 'role versatility'.

Frederick J. McDonald, a learning theorist, has proposed a 'mobile education' that takes the student out of the classroom not merely to observe but to participate in significant community activity. If learning is to be stretched over a life-time, there is reduced justification for forcing kids to attend school full time. Part-time schooling and part-time work, at low-skill paid and unpaid community service tasks, will prove more satisfying and educational.

As levels of education rise, more and more parents are intellectually equipped to assume some responsibilities now delegated to the schools. Quite a few parents are clearly more capable of teaching certain subjects to their children than are the teachers in the local schools. So, the educated parents could pull their children at least part-way out of the public education system, offering them home instruction instead. However, students might continue going to school for social and athletic activities, or for subjects they cannot learn on their own, or under the tutelage of their parents or family members.

Besides home, community is an important area where children could undergo meaningful, practical education. Students would be taught skills by adults in the community as well as by regular faculty. Curricula would be shaped by students and community groups as well as professional educators. Some educators suggest bringing the community into the school so that local stores, medical laboratories, advertising agencies, broadcasting stations, printing shops, and other parlours be given free space in the schools in return for free lessons by the adults who run them.

There are others who think in terms of designing secondary and higher education programmes so as to make use of 'mentors' drawn from the adult population. Such mentors consisting of planners, builders, carpenters, accountants, doctors, engineers, businessmen and other professionals, not only transmit skills, but would show how the abstractions of the textbook are applied to life. These skilled workers of the community become part of an outside faculty in a dialectical swing toward a new kind of apprenticeship for the young students.

All these innovations imply changes in instructional techniques as well. Lectures, which still dominate the classroom, must give way to a whole battery of teaching techniques, ranging from role playing and gaming to the immersion of students in 'contrived experiences'. All these changes point to a long overdue breakdown of the factory-model school and pave the way to convert home and community into part-time schools.

8. GOOD CHILDREN'S BOOKS FOR SHAPING PERSONALITY

The present day parents, who are obsessed with the good rank their children should get in the school, are hardly aware of the need for exposing their children to books outside school curriculum. Even if some children are found reading books outside their curriculum, not all parents would appreciate it. They think it is a sheer waste of time and force their children to confine themselves to the prescribed texts so that they will be in a position to pay full attention to their studies and score good marks in the examinations.

Also, how many educationists and teachers are conscious of the fact that books serve other than purely educational or informational functions? Very few have thought of the role that good children's books play in the growth of children who, as future citizens, are going to shape the destinies of the modern world.

Good books meant for children play a vital role in shaping their personality and moulding their thought at a right time. Good children's books could be meaningful in terms of the child's own experience and environment. For instnce, a book, whose hero or heroine is a child, mirrors the child-reader's own image. Child psychologists tell us that it is essential for a child's development to have a mirror in which he can literally see himself. The psychologists further maintain that children who never see themselves in a full-length mirror grow up lacking a full sense of their own unique personality.

Serving as their mirror images, good children's books enable the children to see children like themselves. Going through the experiences of childhood, the children can view their own lives and surroundings with more objective understanding. In this way, children's books help children develop into mature, sensitive human beings.

For centuries together youngsters have simply pre-empted books such as Bunyan's *Pilgrim's Progress*, Swift's *Gulliver's Travels* and Defoe's *Robinson Crusoe* which were actually written for grown-ups. But, they were our only children's classics.

Children's books have made a late appearance in Indian publishing. Except for the establishment of the non-profit Children's Book Trust, and the appearance of India Book House's *Amar Chitra Katha* which features mythological and folk-tales in the comic book format, commercial houses have until recently dealt only in textbooks and largely continue to rely on them for sales.

But, things have fortunately changed. Some exciting things have been happening during the past decade as efforts are being made to create books by Indian authors with Indian settings and themes for young readers. Most people in the book trade in India are now aware of the need to produce for Indian children books that are meaningful in terms of their own experience and environment, and they are, indeed, doing something about it.

For instance, the Vikas Publishing House has a special department committed to producing a wide range of well-researched, well-produced books mostly in the notification category for youngsters upto 15 years. Thomson Press Children's Books Division is producing painting books based on Indian art and sculpture and Indian Folk-tale collections. Then, the National Book Trust, a Government of India undertaking, is bringing out children's books in regional Indian languages. All the books are brightly illustrated, by well-known artists to make them attractive as supplementary reading material in school, and are priced at levels children can readily afford. Thus, we have a growing band of publishers who cater to children and who are dedicated to children becoming future readers through contact with quality books.

The themes of these children's books range from contemporary problems to informative dynamics on a wide range of subjects — mountaineering, Indian rivers, postage stamps, bird watching, theatre, sports, railways, world-famous inventions and the Indian freedom movement. The authors of these books are particularly concerned with giving the Indian child an image of himself which is no less than the image he conceives of the English and American youth who have so far his only fictional models. On top of that, the use of suitable language and appropriate images in art work offers the child-reader adventures in which he can 'see' himself.

But, the crux of the problem is the general lack of awareness in India of the importance of non-text book reading to a child's growth. It is high time parents, teachers and educational authorities realised the importance of exposing children to non-text book reading. The parents must somehow manage to spare some money for the purchase of some good and interesting books their children would love to read. The teachers should impress upon the young students not to confine themselves to the prescribed text books and encourage them to read as many books and magazines as possible outside the curriculum. The educational authorities would do well to equip the libraries of schools with good children's books. This would go a long way in heightening the awareness of the role of books in a child's development. It is not for nothing that it is said that 'a society is all right when it offers children a choice of books in rich abundance'.

9. INTELLIGENCE TESTS FOR ESTIMATING PUPILS LEARNING CAPACITIES

Anyone who examines an individual's adjustment to life's problems is bound to note that his intelligence shows some direct relationships. People of higher intelligence can handle problems which are beyond the capacities of those of lower intelligence.

Some investigators think that the intelligence of an individual is probably fixed at birth, and certain ones believe that it is determined even before birth through heredity. Whatever its basic origin may be, a person's intelligence quotient, as measured by various I.Q. tests, may vary over a span of years. In general, however, the range in which an individual falls usually remains fairly constant.

In the field of education, intelligence tests have been useful in estimating the learning capacities of pupils. In this rapidly changing scientific age, no country can afford to lose sight of the importance of bringing up children on strict scientific lines so as to make them worthy citizens. This can be best achieved by devising a method whereby the abilities and the intelligence potential of the children, especially in the 5-15 years age group, are scientifically assessed so that they can be given the type of education that best suits them.

Appraisal of such abilities at a younger age have several advantages. Children who have not attained abilities commensurate with their age level can be identified as 'below average' and suitable remedial measures can be thought of to bring them back to the average level. Special attention can be bestowed on such children. It is a common assumption that gifted children in any class who are considered 'above average' are capable of better assimilation of knowledge while the 'below average' do call for extra effort on the part of the teacher. An awareness that a child is 'below average' gives self-appraisal to the child and leads to evaluation on the part of the teacher and the parents. Such an appraisal will help in properly planning the future career of the child.

Testing of intelligence on scientific lines began in the first decade of the present century in the Western countries. Psychologists used verbal and non-verbal material and devised instruments and techniques that could be administered individually or in groups to measure mental abilities and personality traits. In India too, psychologists and educationists have been aware of these developments and the movement of psychological testing has been gaining ground.

However, intelligence testing in India, as Malcolm S. Adiseshaiah has rightly pointed out, is not sufficient for educational planning and development in the country. He says, "It is necessary in the sense that on the results obtained, the individual student's educational path may be charted and promoted, and educational futures for each tested group of students agreed upon. It is not sufficient in the sense that though the tests show that children from higher castes and those exposed to better schooling facilities consistently perform better than those from scheduled castes and those exposed to inadequate schooling, the answer is not to provide excellent schooling facilities for the latter, because where that was done, the effects on higher caste-scheduled caste disparities in skills were not reduced but accentuated."

This observation should prompt the Government of India to introduce Model Schools in every district under the New Educational Policy. Because the educational disparity which intelligence testing brings out between children of different social groups cannot be remedied simply by education and its skills building system : it calls for extra educational, social-political decisions to correct such disparities emanating from social inequalities.

There is also another problem with intelligence testing in India. This limitation flows from the fact that all the tests known and available have been developed in a cultural context that is non-Indian, as from Europe and the United States. Even within those European and the American tests, the cultural bias is explicitly noted, when using such terms as the 'experimenter's bias', 'ecological correlation' and the most loaded term of all 'genetic difference'. In applying these tests to India, there are not only problems of cultural bias, but also value-loaded issues which tend to be hidden.

In spite of these limitations, intelligence tests are of valuable aid to the educationist as a means of diagnosis of the capacity of pupils. They are also used to educational guidance and vocational selection. Intelligence tests enable us to study the interrelationship of mental traits and to investigate mental types. They also throw light on the question whether individual differences in mental capacity are the effect of heredity or environment, or both. The intelligence tests would enable the teacher to have a thorough grasp of his pupils, their abilities, their limitations and their aspirations in order to make teaching effective and interesting in the classroom.

10. TOWARDS AN ADEQUATE PUPIL EVALUATION

The conventional marking or grading system prevalent in our schools is based upon competition among individuals for marks in a more or less standardized body of subject-matter and learning skills. The usual plan of evaluation, based on the assignment of a specific mark, either on a percentage basis or on the five-point scale in which symbols are used to indicate 'Distinction', 'Good', 'Very Fair', 'Fair', 'Failure', falls far short of being an adequate evaluation programme.

Based purely on competitive achievement, marking or grading often becomes harmful in its psychological effect upon both high-ability and low-ability students. First of all, under a system putting the whole emphasis upon getting high marks, the marks, rather than the studies themselves, tend to become the goals of the pupils. Secondly, the grading system bolsters up poor teaching and an inadequate curriculum. Thirdly, the competitive grading system tends to develop dishonesty because of the heavy pressure put upon the student to get high grades willy-nilly. Lastly, competitive grading tends to set up barriers between teachers and pupils. This is likely to occur primarily in situations where grades are failing or near failing. More often than not, the teacher finds himself explaining and defending the grade rather than engaging himself in improving the learning situation of the pupil.

From this it is clear that the conventional marking system does not present an adequate picture of the characteristics and modification of pupil performance and behaviour. All that it aims at doing is to measure pupils' accomplishment in a standardized body of subject-matter.

But, evaluation is more than measurement. A clear concept of the aim of education is basic to evaluation. And, the programme must be organized and developed to evaluate growth in all those understandings, attitudes, appreciations, and essential abilities which are incorporated in a comprehensive statement of the aims of education. The school must be concerned with the integration of character and personality traits as it is with the so-called three R's. The evaluation programme must also be adjusted to the needs and abilities of the individual.

Adequate evaluation should lead to an improvement of the learning situation. Educators must be concerned not only with what the pupil has learned, but with the continuous improvement of the learning situation. The learning situation in the school becomes a process of setting up aims to be achieved, of planning ways and means of achieving desired ends, and of initiating and carrying on various learning activities.

Lastly, an evaluation programme requires an adequate cumulative record system. Records of growth, maintained over a period of years, are as essential to an evaluation programme as measurement. An adequate record system begins with the pupils entry into school, is cumulative in nature, and covers all phases of the pupil's development. The records must include data on social and emotional as well as physical and intellectual development, and must be based on standardized tests, attitude and adjustment inventories, community activities and organizations, and teacher judgments of capacity in each of the curriculum areas.

II

ENGLISH TEACHING IN INDIA

1. TOWARDS CHANGE OF ATTITUDE TO ENGLISH

The most crucial problem confronting the educationist in the country, the teacher in the classroom and the parent in uncomfortable households is the erosion of quality which is the characteristic of the present day dismal situation of English teaching and learning in India. The malaise that plagues the learning and the teaching of English in our country makes a long and a sad story of our pre-Independence unsound assumptions and post-Independence unrealized expectations.

As a result, teachers of English have, perhaps, been too long inhibited and have suffered from the stigma of having to deal with an alien tongue inherited from the days of our political independence. In the British days, English enjoyed an artificial kind of pride of place and prestige. When we came into our own, English, howsoever discouraged politically, began to assert its usefulness. Even so, we are exhorted today to regard English strictly as a 'library' language, and as a 'tool' subject or some such hybrid phenomenon — a creature that needs an excuse for its being and must ask leave to exercise its permitted function. What is, therefore, most called for is a refreshing change of attitude to the teaching and learning of English.

First of all, our acceptance of English language and literature are to be wholly free and uninhibited. English should be regarded as one of the languages of this country of many diverse cultures and ethnic affiliations, and not a foreign language any more. Just in the way a language like Urdu, for instance, evolved and became one of our languages as a result of historical events, so might English, 'this distant covering of the Indo-European family', claim a domicile here having married and settled down. English then would simply be an aspect of that peculiar diversification that is built into our national life, an essential feature of the many-faced Indian identity.

Such a 'free' acceptance of English would have several implications. The process of its naturalization on our soil must mean that English will come to terms with us as much as we will come to terms with it. That oppressive phonological 'watch and ward officer' called R.P. will have to be retired on long leave or else 'translated' in the Bully Bottom sense. That is, perhaps, a trifle.

The more important thing, however, is to regard English as more than a language, very much more. English could be, as has already been, a transforming force — the carrier of a dynamic principle which can renew our whole social fabric and stimulate the individual's initiative. English might be looked upon as the proverbial 'leaven' that can set up the much needed ferment and new growth. As a people who are sure of ourselves, and sure of the firmness of our roots, we need not fear change and renewal. We can still look for that short of epochal upsurge, a people stirred to fresh enterprize for a great new beginning.

Also, the traditional approach to English as a literary and humanistic instrument of liberal education has to willy-nilly undergo a basic change because of the pressure and relevance of new objective suited to the needs of the changed situation and the current requirements of a vast number of Indian students. English must serve individual, social and natural needs as these could be identified in the present day context of our educational and planning priorities. In its diverse national needs at higher levels, English must play various constructive and educative roles such as a language of development, a medium for science and technology, a link language and a language for various opportunities for employment.

And it should be the task of the teacher of English to equip the student with this linguistic attainment by following modern, need-based syllabi and improved methods of teaching English. Furthermore, the teachers of English have to come into their own and dare to be innovative in all the spheres of their vocation. They have to learn and teach how to use English with complete fidelity to their Indian identity so that they are in the mainstream of our regenerative movement, not merely playing a peripheral role. All this implies that our English should mesh with the truth of our experience without falsification.

2. MAKING TEACHING OF ENGLISH AT THE SECONDARY LEVEL MORE MEANINGFUL

While we all seem to acknowledge the steep fall in the standards of English, very few of us ever bother to know what exactly has gone wrong with the teaching or study of English in our schools and colleges. It is at the Secondary School level that the foundations for learning English are laid. And, ironically enough, it is at the Secondary level that the teaching of English is most neglected.

Even at the Secondary School level, in regard to other subjects and language, only specialists are allowed to teach. For instance, only a Science graduate can teach science. Even to teach the mother tongue, Telugu, Tamil or Kannada, there are Telugu 'pandits' in every High School to teach Hindi. But, to teach a foreign language like English, it is stupefying to note, there are no English 'pandits' who have specialised in teaching English as a foreign language to Indian students.

It is high time this gross anomaly was noticed and remedied. It is at the High School level that the foundations for learning English are laid. And it is during this period that the student, young, enthusiastic, energetic, but immature, needs utmost care, right direction and proper coaching in his attempt to learn and master English. And only a competent teacher who has a mastery over English structures, patterns, usage and syntax can deliver the goods and satisfy the requirements of the English teacher at the Secondary School level. For, the main aim of teaching English at the Secondary School stage is to enable the student to acquire language skills — a reasonable mastery of the 200 or so basic structures of English, a vocabulary extending to about 3000 frequent and useful words and an intelligible pronunciation.

The teaching of English in High School continues to change rapidly even in the West where English happens to be the mother tongue of the students. Among the many recent developments are the increased stress on improvisation, dramatisation, the tendency towards teaching rich English language content rather than only grammar and usage, greater freedom in the range of literary materials, greatest emphasis on the process of writing, and the formulation of objectives stated in terms of what the student does rather than in terms of abstract content. These are precisely the lines on which the teaching of English at the Secondary School level in India should be shaped and moulded.

Again pronunciation is one that is sadly neglected in the teaching of English. When education was mainly through English, pronunciation was learnt through imitation, and since no one imitated a model exactly, each generation spoke English worse than the last. This should be remedied by paying attention to pronunciation in teaching. This could be done by giving teachers necessary training in phonetics and spoken English.

Fortunately for us there are institutes like the Central Institute of English in Hyderabad, and the Regional Institutes of English in cities like Calcutta and Bangalore which are run on very sound lines, and in which excellent training in teaching English as a foreign language is offered by way of short term as well as long term courses leading to the award of Certificates and Diplomas. But, it is unfortunate that a Diploma from such institutes is not made a pre-requisite for the English teacher in High Schools.

Every care should, therefore, be taken to create proper atmosphere for the teaching of English at the Secondary School level. First of all, only those who are fully competent to teach English as a foreign language to Indian students should be appointed as English teachers. In view of the special problems and natural difficulties involved in teaching English unlike in teaching Indian languages, it is highly desirable to choose Post-graduates who have specialised in teaching English as a foreign language to native students. Besides theoretical methods, proper use should be made of visual and a aural aids. For this a simple language laboratory, which is not beyond the reach of Secondary School education, is necessary. All this, however, will be of no avail unless and until the strength in each class is restricted to not more than forty so that there could be individual attention of the teacher on each student which is imperative at this stage. Only then can we hope to see young boys and girls attaining good standards of English which will stand them in good stead not only when they go for higher education later, but also when they seek any job soon after their matriculation.

3. INDIAN-ENGLISH TEXTS AS ENGLISH-TEACHING MATERIAL

The traditional view is that it is better to learn English from an Englishman's English or an American's English than from an Indian's English. Most Indian teachers of English subscribe to this view and generally resist the idea of using Indian writing in English as English-teaching material for Indians. Small wonder, therefore, if the anthologies of prose, poetry and short stories prescribed for study at the Intermediate and Degree levels are dominated by non-Indian writers.

Paradoxically enough, the same teachers have no hesitation in teaching English as a full-time and life-long profession. What is more, they assess others' competence in English, write books on English grammar and usage, discuss the subtleties of English literary texts and do a number of things which contradict their mistrust in the classroom of a text composed in English by a fellow Indian.

What we have to realize is that where the main purpose is to teach the English language, the national origin of the writer does not matter so long as the English he has used is grammatically correct, lexically varied and stylistically interesting in composing a text that is intellectually as well as artistically valid. As a matter of fact, when grammar, lexi and syntax are at work upon a culture-content that is familiar to the Indian student, such material would prove more malleable as a teaching text than an essay by Robert Lynd or a sketch by G.K. Chesterton or a poem by T.S. Eliot.

The great advantage an Indian-English text enjoys in our classrooms over any British or American text is that the student has direct access to the culture surrounding the text, even outside the classroom. He can be persuaded to see the text not only as something printed on a page but as something related to him in real life as well. When the culture connotations of a text pose no barriers, the learner can grapple directly with the language of the text.

This point is seldom conceded to by those who are in favour of British/American English texts. They argue that in learning a foreign language one also learns, about a foreign culture, and that the two processes supplement and reinforce each other. This is not untrue. But the point is that the whole process of learning the English language would be facilitated if the Indian student were to learn the English language on familiar grounds before approaching unfamiliar contexts through it. Hence, the desirability of learning English preferably through an Indian-English text.

Original creative writing in English by Indians is a relatively recent growth, no older than the last one hundred years. So, it is relatively limited in quantity and variety. But, we can certainly depend upon the resources of Indian writing in English translation which, if properly developed and cultivated, would be quite exhaustive. It could draw upon the creative writing of any age in more than a dozen languages. A great advantage that can be squeezed out of the translation situation is by obliging the student, at all stages of his education, to carry out exercises in translation from his own language into English. This will be part of his English language learning. He is brought very close to the literary process itself, and an aspiring student of literature is bound to gain a lot from the practical experience of translation.

From the terminal years of school upto the first degree level, those doing compulsory English or opting for General English could be nourished on a wide variety of translated material — narrative fiction both short and long, lyric poetry and plays of reasonable length. At a later stage, it may also be possible to use verse translations of ancient and medieval narrative poems of manageable length. Thus, English translations of Indian writing can be used as an instrument to 'bring the distant near and make a brother of the stranger'.

Furthermore, in a country as old and large as India, literary material is the handiest means of learning something about the rest of the country, its time, its space and, above all, its cultural heritagte. So, learning English through an Indian-English text, original or translation, provides general education to the student. No opportunity must be lost of using the classroom to widen the literary culture of our school and college-going youth and make them aware of the magnitude of our literary heritage.

Therefore, without seeking to subvert our firmly entrenched instruments for teaching English, we should start using Indian writing in English as an experimental alternative to British/American texts that have been our staple for so long.

III

MODERN METHODS OF LEARNING

1. PROGRAMMED LEARNING

The complexities of modern education and industrial training require the application of all our understanding of instructional techniques so that the limited number of teachers and instructors will be able to provide the most thorough instruction possible for the ever-increasing number of students. Programmed learning is one of the latest instructional techniques which comes handy to meet the challenges that education in India poses at present.

Programmed learning is a process of constructing sequences of instructional material in a way that maximises the rate and depth of learning, fosters understanding and enhances the motivation of students. The subject-matter of a programme is presented into logical sequence of small steps. The small steps emphasize the gradual nature of the increase in complexity and the smoothness of the transition from one item to the next. Programmed learning takes every care to teach the student to make discriminations among the range of possibilities and to educe generalizations or to make extensions from given data to new situations.

Programmed learning has taken roots from the application of basic principles of learning such as stimuli and responses, transfer of stimulus control, prompting and guided discovery, gradual progression, reinforcement, generalisation and discrimination, concept formation and successive approximations developed in the laboratories of psychology. Responding appropriately to certain stimuli and doing it according to an appropriate sequence is all that knowledge means.

Programmed learning is making headway at a tremendous speed with various styles of programming — Linear programming, Branching programming, Mathetics, and Learner-controlled instruction. Programmers have experimented with these styles and have tried to assess the learning potentiality of each one of them.

In Linear programme the learner has no choice of his own in following the path or sequence of learning. It is decided extrinsically by the linear programmer who sets out to make each successive step in his programme small enough to avoid error from the learner. Since the steps are small, a linear programme moves slowly in an inevitable progress towards its terminal behaviour.

Branching programme is based on traditional tutorial methods. The student usually responds by indicating his answer to a multiple-choice question, and if he makes errors he is given remedial help. The student's response provides feedback to the programme on whatever he managed to communicate.

The Mathetical technique discusses procedures for analysing the terminal behaviour to be taught, and for planning the sequence of instruction. The learner performs all the operations that will be required of him, learning by doing. Sequences or chains in which each response sets up a unique stimulus state of affairs are taught backwards.

The Learner-controlled instruction approach puts proper emphasis upon the learner as the central focus of the teacher-learner relationship. It is based on the fact that the teacher exists for the learner, not *vice versa*, unless the teacher is primarily a performer whose ego must be fed daily. The method reiterates that the learner deserves consideration both as one who has experience which can possibly be used as basis towards unerstanding, and as one who, in most cases, is not completely without resourcefulness.

Programmed learning places a great responsibility on the programmer in the sense that he has to understand the various intricacies of the subject he intends to programme as well as the promises of various styles of programming. He must be ingenuous with a knack for imaginative and creative work. What is more, he must have a scientific inclination to study the nature of behaviour, its various forms and levels.

It is now very rightly claimed that programmed learning is making the students more critical of the learning process and more aware of what is heppening to make them learn. Controlled experiments have shown that a good programme can achieve the same results as a good classroom teacher, usually in less time. It may be safely asserted that programmed learning can free the teacher from the course of routine instruction, exercise setting and remarking. The teacher can spend more and more of his time in giving individual guidance and special help.

2. CO-OPERATIVE LEARNING

Co-operative learning is an old Indian concept in education which has undergone a substantial revival in educational research and practice in the past few years, especially in the West. The term, co-operative learning, refers to classroom techniques in which students work on learning activities in small groups and receive rewards or recognition based on their group's performance.

A remarkable upsurge in research has taken place in recent years on the academic, attitudinal and social-interactive effects of co-operative school learning in teams. This research has sought to assess the effectiveness of several specific team-learning methods for promoting academic achievement, positive school-related attitudes and ethnic integration in the desegregated classroom.

The bulk of the research on practical co-operative learning techniques has focused on three major models — Student Teams-Achievement Divisions, Jigsaw, and Small-Group Teaching. All these methods employ small teams of pupils to promote peer interaction and co-operation for studying academic subjects.

Student Teams-Achievement Divisions uses 4 to 5 members heterogeneous teams with simple 15 minute puzzles which students take after studying in their teams. The quiz scores are translated into team scores using a system called 'achievement divisions'. The quiz scores of the highest six students in past performance are compared, and the top scorer earns eight points for his group, the second scorer earns six points and so forth. Then, the quiz scores of the next highest six students in past performance are compared and so on. In this way, student scores are compared only with those of an ability—homogenous reference group instead of the entire class.

In Jigsaw, students are assigned to small heterogeneous teams as in Student Teams-Achievement Divisions. Academic material is broken into as many sections as there are team members. For example, a biography might be broken into 'early years', 'schooling', 'first accomplishments', 'failure encounters' and so on. The students study their sections with members of other teams who have the same sections. Then, they return to their teams and teach their sections to the other team members. Finally, all team members are quizzed as the entire unit.

Small-Group Teaching is a general classroom organizational plan in which learning takes place through co-operative group enquiry, discussion and date-gathering by students. Students select sub-topics within a general area selected by the teacher, and then organize themselves into small groups of two to six members. These groups would further sub-divide their topic into individual tasks to be performed by group members in preparation for a group presentation to the total class. Thus, Small-Group Teaching is very high in student autonomy and involves a high degree of task independence. This is because of the assignment of students to special tasks within the group. It is, however, to be noted that Small-Group Teaching is relatively low in group reward interdependence.

The outcome of co-operative learning falls mainly into two categories — academic achievement and group cohesiveness. The effects of the techniques on the group cohesiveness variables such as mutual concern and race relations are unquestionably positive. The academic achievement results, though also usually positive, seem to depend on the particular techniques, setting, measures, experimental designs or other characteristics. Thus, there is ample evidence from field research to support the use of co-operative learning in schools. It is time Indian schools tried co-operative learning thereby reviving an old Indian system in a modern scientific way.

3. TOWARDS SELF-DIRECTED LEARNING

Generally, we think of learning as something that occurs in an educational institution under the direction of a teacher, within the structure of a course based upon textbooks, and evaluated by a written examination. Though most common, this is a narrow view of learning and education. We learn formally as well as informally, but what we learn informally through a self-directed process is likely to be more effective with a higher degree of retention and assimilation.

Nevertheless, schools and colleges and other institutions of learning encourage students to be dependent, passive, conforming and generally willing to be directed. Therefore, a way of helping students of all ages to become skilfully self-directed must be found and made a part not just of schooling but of all forms of education, including the education parents give their children and the education that all of us give ourselves throughout our lives. Not for nothing a psychologist said, "All education is self-education in the same way that all jumping is high-jumping."

Pupils spend more time out of school than in it even on a school day, let alone in a year or during the tenure of their studentship. What is more, when the school and college days end, even the best educated have forty or fifty years of life and learning still ahead of them. And continued growth during these out-of-school hours and years requires continued learning — learning to master new jobs, to play new roles to open new dimensions in ourselves and in our relationships, and to make contributions worthy of our capacities.

Such growth or informal, self-directed learning is significantly different from formal education. In self-directed learning the individual masters all the activities usually conducted by the teacher — selecting goals, organizing learning experiences, evaluating progress and redesigning strategies for greater effect. The self-educator tends to develop his expertise through active, experiential, self-directed, situational, and often challenging means rather than the passive, abstract, theoretical, teacher-directed means which often occur in a classroom situation where the challenge is predictable and controlled.

Recent psychologists have offered viewpoints as well as various techniques for personalizing education and for teaching people to teach themselves. George Isaac Brown (1972), for instance, describes ways to make academic learning a personal experience. Alan Tough analyses the nature and process of self-directed learning. Edgar Faure, Chairman of the UNESCO Committee, in his book, *Learning to Be* (1972), concludes that education must combine practical experience with academic studies and it must do this in a way that promotes self-education and prepares people for life-long-learning.

Recent developments in both behaviorist and humanistic psychology are also potential contributions to self-education theory. Russell Hill and Herbert Benson demonstrate the broad spectrum of beneficial effects that accompany deep relaxation and meditation, pointing to the potential usefulness of 'Yoga' and other Eastern disciplines of mind to self-education. They also describe various ways to teaching people to plan their own programmes of action, feedback and reinformcement.

It is essential to take note of the basic principles of self-education and their implications for teaching. Teaching for self-education involves integrating theoretical studies with technical training and practical application and helping students generate their own drive towards their own goals rather than stimulating them to pursue goals set for them by others. Teaching for self-education should promote the development of personal integrity rather than opportunistic pursuit of offered rewards, of self-discipline rather than obedience, of inner drive rather than passivity, of independence rather than dependence, of originality rather than conformity, and finally help each student develop a personal learning style.

4. THE VALUE OF DISCUSSION

Discussion occupies an important place in learning procedure particularly at the collegiate and university levels. Discussion may be defined as "an activity characterised by adherence to a topic, question or problem about which the participants sincerely wish to arrive at a decision". In discussion, which is to be relevant and meaningful, one arrives at a conclusion through analysis, comparison and evaluation. It is highly desirable to have a discussion after completing a subject in the class.

Discussions could be held in various ways. The teacher himself can introduce the topic, give some points and put it forward for discussion. The teacher can also call upon a student to come forward with a suitable topic and he gives some guidelines and gets a discussion started. Or, the teacher and the student may co-operatively prepare a brief outline of points which can form the basis of discussion. Another method of discussion is that special reports by experts on a particular topic could be furnished and the class could be asked to discuss them with a view to arriving at a definite conclusion.

There are various types of discussions — group discussion, panel discussion, roundtable discussion, open forums and symposia. While each type of discussion is good in its own way, it cannot be chosen at random. The type of discussion to be chosen depends upon the nature of the topic, meant for discussion. Group discussions, however, are more frequently used than others, And, symposium is, perhaps, the most popular kind of group discussion in academic circles.

A symposium is a form of group discussion in which the participants may present to the audience through speeches or paper-reading their views on various phases of a selected problem or topic which is usually a controversial one. The main advantage of a symposium is that many students can take part in it and express their views. The purpose of a symposium is to supply definite information which is needed by the class to solve a particular problem or understand a topic.

So, the topic of the symposium should be chosen carefully with the co-operation of the students. It should be meaningful and of educational value. The teacher or a student presides over the symposium and another student introduces the topic. The teacher should evaluate the results of the symposium. the symposia prove to be very helpful in clarifying thoughts upon controversial problems.

The teacher's role in discussions is very important. First and foremost, he must secure the co-operation of the entire class. He should see that the subject chosen is relevant and the approach is interesting. It is also his duty to see that the important points are covered in discussion, heated arguments are avoided and only interpretations are given, and that all the students are drawn into the discussion. The teacher should also stimulate the students' mental activity and inform them of the sources from where they can get information needed to sustain the discussion.

Furthermore, the teacher's guidance at every phase is important. The teacher has a great responsibility to see that the discussion 'keeps on the track', and does not become too academic or stereotyped. He should never embarrass any student. He should encourage the timid and make each student feel that he has contributed something to the discussion. Under any circumstances, the discussion should not be allowed to be monopolised by a single student or a group of students. Also, it is very necessary that a teacher should know ways and means of handling possible conflicts and for reducing tensions that affect good human relationships.

5. TUTORIALS : A CORRECTIVE TO STUDENT MASS CONTACT

A major defect of the present system of education in India is the lack of proper contact between the teacher and the taught, in glaring contrast to the 'gurukula' system of the past. Now, a crowded class-room has become the only place of learning. The teacher and the student scarcely meet outside the classroom and they hardly know each other, let alone having proper understanding between them. The only means of formal instruction are lectures. Since the classes are overcrowded it has become almost impossible for the teacher to know his students and to see that his lecture is followed by all of them.

However good and useful are lectures, students cannot derive the maximum benefit from them. They are left to themselves and they feel frustrated. This accounts for the poor academic performance on the part of a vast majority of students, especially those who come from rural areas without good educational background.

Hence, the need to supplement lectures by tutorials which provide a corrective to mass contact of students by way of securing individual attention which is very essential for making teaching and learning effective. Although the importance of tutorials has been emphasised by the Radhakrishanan Commission (1948) and the Education Commission (1964-66), it is a pity that they are yet to be implemented properly in almost every institution of higher learning, barring Central Universities. No doubt, a few colleges include tutorials in their teaching schedule but, more often than not, the scheme does not go beyond. It is high time speical attention was paid to proper implementation of tutorials in our colleges and universities.

Tutorials ought to be implemented following a systematic procedure. The lecturer concerned has to announce the subject well in advance recommending the books and journals which provide the material needed. The student collects material from the available sources and then writes an essay on the given subject, and submits it to the teacher-tutor. The teacher evaluates the essay and enters into a discussion with the student. In course of the discussion, the student comes to know of his lapses, defends his viewpoints and also willingly accepts constructive modifications and suggestions by the teacher-tutor on being convinced.

This whole process of reading, thinking, writing, listening, discussing and accepting modifications would go a long way in improving the academic standards of students. The teacher-tutor plays the role of an intellectual catalyst to bring out the original ideas of the students. Thus, tutorials help the students to think for themselves by stimulating their powers of critical analysis of a given problem. This is, indeed, the need of the hour.

Apart from making the students regularly prepare for the university examinations, the tutorials encourage a sense of responsibility for error and a capacity for self-expression. The tutorial system makes the student meaningfully pursue an idea to its logical conclusion thereby developing in him a critical bent of mind which is awfully lacking in the present day education system.

The importance of tutorials as a corrective to mass contact would be realized more in the field of language subjects. Even after graduation many of our students are not in a position to write a few sentences in English correctly. This is mainly due to the lack of opportunities for students to come to know of their own lapses and mistakes in writing through a personal dialogue and living contact with their teachers. The tutorial system can hopefully remedy this academic malady which is a sad commentary on higher education in India. As a limited member of students will be allotted to each language teacher, he would be in a position to carefully go through the scripts submitted to him and correct his mistakes. He can also explain to the students the means and ways to improve their linguistic skills.

The scheme of tutorials can suitably be of a three-tier at the undergraduate level. In the first year of the Three-year Degree Course, tutorials could be devoted to guided reading and training in independent thinking. In the second year the tutorials can lay emphasis on comparative study and discussion, and .in the final year on critical analysis and assessment.

The tutorials can play a more vital role at the post-graduate level where the student is expected to depend more and more on himself. To be effective, the tutorials should form an integral part of post-graduate education. The teacher concerned can suggest the relevant topics on which the student prepares essays and short notes drawing on what he has learnt in the classroom and, more importantly, what he has gathered from the books and journals in the university library. This makes the student go to the university library and consult the relevant books and journals which are hardly made use of at present. Libraries will no longer be museums but pulsate with intellectual activity. Books and journals will no longer gather dust, but shine with intellectual light shed on them by the inquisitive and curious student propelled by the tutorial system. Each student should be made to submit at least one assignment every week. These assignments need not be confined to the prescribed syllabus but extended to cover the latest trends in the field of knowledge concerned. After a proper evaluation of the submitted assignments the teacher can have a meaningful dialogue with the student and give suggestions for improvement of both the matter and method of presentation.

There should be at least one tutorial for each subject in a week. Tutorials should form a part of the time-table and be held regularly.

Teachers should shun their indifference and step-motherly attitude to tutorials and give them their due importance. The Boards of Studies of each discipline in the university should become alive to the increasing importance of tutorials and formulate the norms of the tutorial system, for its implementation. Certain percentage of marks can also be allotted to the assignments submitted by students regularly with a view to motivating them to take to tutorials with interest and zeal. Properly implemented, the scheme of tutorials would go a long way in providing the much needed corrective to the present mass contact of students.

IV

CHANGING ROLE OF UNIVERSITIES

1. FROM 'IVORY TOWERS' TO 'DREAMING SPIRES'

Right from the beginning, the object of universities has been the transmission of the hard-won knowledge and wisdom of the past to succeeding generations as well as the discovery of new knowledge and new wisdom that would raise man's status. Thus, universities have been geared to liberate human minds, stir the imagination and cultivate the sensibilities of individual human beings.

The purpose of university education has been the enlargement of individual opportunity and enrichment of individual life. One went to the university to better oneself. Whether it also enriched the lives of others and contributed to community welfare was incidental, and depended on the uses to which the individual graduate or post-graduate put his knowledge and learning. By and large, the university in the past has suffered from too much detachment with the result that it had little impact on the work-a-day world.

Within the last few years, however, we have entered on a new dimension in the relationship of the university and community. The intensifying application of technical and scientific knowledge to human affairs has made an immense contribution to productivity and material welfare. This has brought about a breathtaking rate of social change which alters the relationship of the univeristy to the community in many ways.

The university has to be a public service institution. Who goes to a university and what is taught there have become matters of much wider public concern than ever before. The individualistic age has ended and given rise to a collectivist age. All sorts of goals are now determined collectively instead of being left for individuals to discern and achieve.

Furthermore, the universities which are inescapably dependent on large government grants for operating purposes will have to come to terms. Coming to terms, however, does not mean governmental control of what is taught in universities and how. The universities must be able to retain enough freedom about the way in which they study and teach the subjects they must teach. For instance, a university may be obliged to educate doctors or produce engineers, but be left free to decide what to teach them and how.

Thus, social pressures, on the one hand, and governmental influence, on the other, have resulted in bringing the university and the community to closer relationship than ever before. So, the universities could no longer be mere seats of learning. They are answerable to the public.

The universities should exert a vital influence on society. The way to have a vital role in a society is to be immersed in it, subjected to its pressures, and be sensitive to its deeply felt needs. Utter detachment from the hustle of one's society is a resignation from life, wanted only by those who shrink from facing life. The ivory tower which has been an imposing structure on Indian universities is now to be shattered to pieces. Insofar as the ivory tower is a rejection of all concerned with the matters that agitate the society of the day, we can say that its fate is sealed.

We can forget about the 'ivory towers' but must, at all costs, preserve the 'dreaming spires' which are symbolic of high, unhurried and contemplative thought. It would still be possible for penetrating and fertile minds to withdraw periodically from all the clamour of the immediate for thought and reflection on the things they themselves think worth pursuing. The university professor's public service role should also permit him to persist in unpromising lines of inquiry such as the splitting of the atom was once popularly believed to be, or to pursue other seemingly unprofitable inquiries in literature, philosophy and history. In spite of his commitment to the community welfare, the university teacher shall have time for independent study of his subject so as to ensure that he keeps himself alive in it.

To sum up, in a developing country like India, if there are to be universities worthy of the name, they should bid farewell to their 'ivory towers' and be oriented to community development, preserving at the same time their 'dreaming spires'. Their resources and dispositions must encourage thinking of this order. For, from it alone comes all the winning of genuinely new ground for the map of knowledge and the insights that make classrooms and laboratories stirring places.

2. MAKING RESIDENTIAL LIFE OF UNIVERSITY STUDENTS MORE PURPOSEFUL

Man is essentially a social being and, therefore, mutual education is one of the great and incessant occupations of human society. Every man, right from infancy, owes more than can possibly be estimated to his fellow-creatures. Why, for that matter, our very outlook on life is coloured by what we get from social intercourse than from what we derive from books.

Yet, how many of us realize that a university is first and foremost a corporation, a place of concourse whither students come from various quarters to learn mostly by the very personal contacts with each other as well as with their teachers. We only tend to regard the study of books, attendance at lectures, the passing of examinations and getting the degrees as the chief components of a university life.

We do not seem to be sufficiently aware of the great many benefits which students necessarily derive from intercourse among themselves. As Newman has rightly pointed out long back, "When a multitude of young men, keen, open-hearted, sympathetic and observant, as young men are, come together and freely mix with each other, they are sure to learn from one other, even if there be no one to teach them; the conversation of all is a series of lectures to teach, and they gain for themselves new ideas and views, fresh matter of thought, and distinct principles for judging and acting, day by day."

It is, therefore, very essential that universities in our country should be organized on the basis of personal communication between students. No doubt, in most of the universities provision is made for suitable residential quarters for students. The hostel system must not be regarded as a mere practical convenience, but as a most potential source of mutual education. Because meaningful social intercourse between a large body of students differing in character and taste, in attainment and ambition, congregated together in the pursuit of knowledge is the very nucleus of university life.

It is high time more attention was paid to the residential life of university students and more and more opportunities created for working in intimate and constant association with their fellow-students. The 'enlargement of mind', which every student must acquire, comes not so much from books or lectures as from that intimate personal contact with his fellows. For, as the students come from very different places and with widely different notions, there is much to generalize, much to adjust, much to eliminate, and much to learn from each other, in the process by which the mind is enlarged and the heart is softened.

Once the universities recognize the far-reaching improtance of social intercourse in the learning process of students, and lay as much emphasis on informal education as on formal education, they would be in a position to send out students who are well fitted to meet the challenges of life confidently and successfully. In such ideal universities, if some students do not make a mark in academic work, and even if by any chance they fail to obtain a degree it cannot be held that they have gained nothing by their residence at a university nor that their education has been a failure or waste of time. For, what more is expected of a university education than properly preparing the student to live well facing life with full confidence and cheer thereby giving his best to the world.

3. ENLARGING STUDENT PARTICIPATION IN UNIVERSITY LIFE

The emergence of militant student movements resulting in strikes and gheraos has become the order of the day, causing considerable alarm both to the educational authorities and the governments. The traditional practice has been either to suppress the violent turn or to succumb to its excruciating threats.

If, on the other hand, there can exist effective agencies within the institutional set up to deal with the deficiencies of the educational system whereby the rampant student unrest could be arrested, the present trend of the student body to depend on violence as a measure of self-help will be rendered unnecessary. Thus, if the forces of self-discipline have to emerge from within, the principle of self-government in regard to students will have to be accepted whereby educational institutions can become more democratic and dynamic. The students certainly need more opportunities to take decisions, shoulder responsibilities and practise democratic procedure thereby to develop proper leadership qualities.

Traditionally the serious defect of educational institutions has been the overlooking of the basic premise that the university is a living community comprising students, teachers and administrators. Excluding the students altogether, the administrators in league with some teachers have been framing policies and taking decisions that governed the academic life of students. Nothing could be more ironical than this system inasmuch as it eliminates the involvement of the very persons for whom it is primarily meant.

At present, student participation in the university life amounts to more than students assuming a passive role in co-curricular activities such as debating competitions, cultural shows and sports. But the time has come when we must necessarily enlarge the acope of student participation so as to make it something richer and more meaningful than it is today through the proper organisation of student governments in the universities.

The student government plays a major role in shaping the life on campus through its numerous academic and social activities. The objectives of student government are :

(i) facilitating communication among various segments of the campus;

(ii) increasing the student's identification with the college and his feeling of personal responsibility for learning and development by involving him in making decisions about collegiate life and behaviour;

(iii) providing experience and participation in self-government as a part of citizenship and leadership training; and

(iv) providing a method for meaningfully relating various student activities to each other.

The value of student government arises from the educative function it seeks to perform. The existing classroom experiences which revolve around pure academic goals hardly provide an adequate educative environment. Active participation of students in the life of the university through the organisation of student government provides them certain basic experiences and situations which are necessary for developing certain qualities like (a) a critical bent of mind; (b) a positive attitude to democratic leadership; (c) a spirit of working together with others for common goals; (d) a sense of commitment in life; (e) a sensitivity to the needs of others; and above all, (f) a sense of responsibility for the happiness and suffering of others. These are precisely the qualities that would go a long way in making a well-adjusted, self-disciplined and integrated personality of the university student which is the need of the hour.

4. EMPLOYMENT BUREAUX AS INTEGRAL PART OF UNIVERSITY EDUCATION

In olden days, parents, teachers and elders were guiding the young in social, cultural, moral as well as in professional field. Especially the teacher was a 'guru' guiding the student in all disciplines of life. Now, with the increasing number of colleges and students on the one hand, and the growing economic, social and cultural revolution on the other, guidance cannot possibly be left alone to teachers, parents and elders. It is now a highly specialized subject requiring a planned and organized programme for a continuous study of the complex problem.

With a view to providing a regular and co-ordinated agency for occupational information, guidance and placement service to the increasing population of young students, the Government set up Employment Information and Guidance Bureaux in the universities in 1958. A staff member, usually a professor, serves as part-time Director of each bureau, and the Ministry of Labour provides a full-time employment officer. It has an Advisory Committee too, consisting of Deans of faculties, Principals of colleges and important employers in the area.

But, the mechanical and formal way in which these Employment Bureaux are functioning at present calls for a more realistic and meaningful approach to meet the devouring demands of employment. In the first instance, the Employment Bureaux should no longer be considered separate entities in themselves, just for registering the names of the graduates and passing on employment information to them from the employers. They should necessarily be regarded as an integral part of university education so that they may rise above mere referral agencies and become places of realistic, vocational guidance.

The Employment Bureaux can render a valuable service to the student body not only by offering them vocational information but also by educating them in all placement matters and opportunities through effective counselling and proper guidance. They can help the young student think objectively about his vocational goals and correct any misunderstanding the student may have concerning placement opportunities. They can facilitate his decision about the right choice of a job. They can teach him the art of taking an interview. At the time of the registration itself the employment officer can enlighten the student on various possible employment avenues, realistic approach to salary expectations and long range prospects. Besides individual counselling, group guidance could be provided by means of career talks to homogenous groups of students by employers, specialists and eminent persons from industry, commerce and other disciplines of work.

In addition to counselling and guidance techniques used in assisting a student to analyse his experience, education, training, interests, aptitude and his social or economic situation and equipping him with occupational information relating to various fields of work, the Employment Bureaux could use a number of other specific methods to make their existence more and more meaningful. First of all, they should conduct special orientation programmes for students exposing them to various career opportunities, working conditions, pay scales, methods of recruitment and selection. Besides, career information room at the Bureau can be set up so as to encourage students to read and get information related to their interests. Similarly, assistance could be extended to the colleges affiliating to universities to set up career and promote guidance services. Periodical guidance bulletins containing information on current employment opportunities, scholarships, apprenticeships, training facilities and articles on guidance and occupational information could be published and circulated among students.

The Employment Bureaux would do well to promote and encourage part-time and vocation employment in the field of students' tentative interests as a means of financial aid. They should suggest means and ways whereby the extra-curricular activities of the college can have vocational significance. Furthermore, they can arrange visits of students to establishments employing university graduates. In a similar way, they can invite and encourage employers to interview students and make selections through the Bureau. Thus, the University Employment Bureaux can bring together students and prospective employers for effective employment of students.

5. VOCATIONALIZATION AT DEGREE LEVEL : WHY AND HOW?

It is heartening to note that the University Grants Commission (UGC) has introduced vocational courses at the degree level in many universities, autonomous and other colleges throughout the country. As per the announcement of the Chairman of the UGC, the Government of India sanctioned Rs. 26 crores to the UGC to fund the programme, to start with. The basic idea is to expose the students to the requirements of the world of work and to make them skilled for specific jobs.

For vocationalization of courses at the undergraduate level, the UGC has been able to identify quite a number of subjects — 13 courses in Arts, Humanities and Social Sciences, 10 in Commerce, Economics and Management, 25 in Sciences and 10 in Engineering and Technology. Equally noteworthy is the range of subjects offered for study and training. These cover a broad specturm : archaeology and museology, office management and secretarial practice, tourism and travel management, computer applications, biotechnology, sericulture, still photography, environment, and water management.

A significant point to be noted in vocationalization of these courses is the built-in component relating to on-the-job-training during the vacations with the support of local employing establishments in order to invest the programme with real back-up strength necessary for its sustenance. What is more, the UGC has tried to ensure downward and upward linkages of the subjects by dovetailing the vocational courses with the higher secondary stage and also leaving much scope to carry forward beyond the three-year degree level.

The vocational course would be one subject in a group offered in the B.A., B.Sc., or B.Com. courses. For example, a subject such as advertising and marketing would be offered in place of politics in history, economics and politics group in B.A., and in a similar way, subjects such as tax planning and secretarial courses. The basic objective is to prepare graduates for employment as also to set up small enterprises with the support of financial institutions.

However attractive all this may look on paper, the crux of the problem hinges on how the apparently laudable UGC plan of vocationalization will lend itself to implementation. First of all, there is every danger of the colleges getting attracted by the lucrative UGC aid of a few lakhs of rupees but later finding it difficult to administer the programme in a sustained fashion.

Secondly, vocational courses at present are less attractive than the conventional courses. Vocationalization at the higher secondary stage has not unfortunately made the impact that was expected on account of several factors. Very few students opt for this *vis-a-vis* the academic stream. Only less than five per cent of the higher secondary students nation-wide have taken to the vocational subjects. The reasons are not far to seek. Parents and their wards express a preference for those subjects which will guarantee white collar jobs. Vocational subjects as they are designed now lack credibility on account of the meagre infrastructure in the schools and the dearth of qualified teachers.

On top of that, while introducing vocational courses at the undergraduate level, the UGC has not envisaged any significant change in the basic structure of the present Three-year Degree Course. As per the UGC's scheme, the students will be required just to choose one vocational subject along with the other two subjects prescribed in the university regulations. Hence, the need to restructure the courses at the Degree level to make vocationalization functional and purposeful.

Today, any conscientious educationist in India can raise a pertinent question whether the knowledge imparted in the universities is socially relevant and meaningful. If the answer is in the negative, there is a need to restructure the existing courses and develop new courses around the needs, problems and the resources of the community. If, however, the answer is found to be affirmative in that the knowledge is meaningful and useful to the society, the academic community should demonstrate it through field projects. Both the answers call for action which, in turn, will have two advantages : (1) teaching, tutorials, and experiments in the laboratories will be supplemented by project work in the field, and (2) application of knowledge (and even teaching through field projects on an inter-disciplinary basis) would provide a feedback for the revision of existing courses and the development of new ones.

Restructuring of courses at the undergraduate level has got to be undertaken with a view to making the first degree courses more relevant to the environment and to the development needs of the community and link education with work/field/practical experience and productivity. The new scheme envisages giving to the students a grounding in four important areas : (a) foundation courses; (b) core courses; (c) applied/projects/field activity with some chosen disciplines, including a study of one or more of them in depth; and (d) involvement in national or social services for the first two years. It is necessary to pursue and expand this programme with greater vigour, to bring about a transformation of the conventional courses at the Degree level.

The restructuring of the existing courses or the introduction of new community-oriented courses would mean recasting of the teaching programme too. The entire teaching programme has to be recast in such a way that ten to twenty per cent of the teaching time of different courses is spent on field projects on a collaborative basis, and this type of teaching is incorporated in the time-table of the colleges or the departments. This task will involve grappling with such questions as : (i) identification of topics under each subject which may be covered through field projects; (ii) identification of similar topics in other subjects which may be taught on a cooperative basis: (iii) identification of field projects; (iv) allotment of time to such teaching; (v) development of teaching materials; (vi) evaluation of work done by the students through field projects; and (vii) assessment of the total impact of imparting or application of knowledge on the community.

Answers to these questions may be found by the Boards of Studies when they make an attempt to list topics in their subjects, select projects, distribute teaching time in the first, second and the third years, organise concurrent or block project work, and examine the implications of such teaching. On an experimental basis, universities might examine the possibility of regrouping optional courses in such a way that at least one out of the three optional papers offered by a student is taught through field projects.

All this obviously implies a good deal of integration and re-grouping of courses at the Degree level. The following combination of courses in sciences, and social sciences would serve the purpose.

1. Sciences :

(i) Mathematics, Physics and Electronics/Applied Physics (Workshop Technology/Machine Shop Practice/Instrumentation); (ii) Botany, Chemistry and Horticulture; (iii) Zoology, Chemistry and Fisheries; (iv) Botany/Zoology, Chemistry and Home Science; (v) Zoology/Chemistry and Applied Nutrition and Public Health; (vi) Micro-biology/Zoology, Botany and Applied Nutrition and Public Health; (vii) Micro-Biology/Chemistry/Bio-Chemistry and Applied Nutrition and Public Health; (viii) Botany/Zoology, Chemistry and Soil Sciences; (ix) Physics, Chemistry and Agro-Chemicals including Fertilizers; (x) Botany, Chemistry and Agro-Chemicals including Fertilizers; (xi) Zoology, Chemistry, Dairy Science; (xii) Botany/Zoology, Chemistry and Plant Protection; (xiii) Biology, Chemistry and Plant Protection (where there is an integrated course in plant protection); (xiv) Biology, Chemistry and Nutrition/Home Science.

2. Social Sciences :

(i) Economics, Commerce and Agricultural Marketing; (ii) Economics, Commerce and Farm Management; (iii) Economics, Commerce and Cooperative Management; (iv) Political Science, Economics and Community Development; (v) History, Political

Science and Local Self-Government; (vi) Economics/Political Scinece, Cultural Anthropology/Sociology of Community Life; (vii) Economics, Political Science and Panchayati Raj; (viii) Economics, Commerce and Rural Industrialization; (ix) Economics, Commerce and Rural Banking; (x) Economics, Sociology and Labour Welfare; (xi) Economics, Sociology and Insustrial Relations; (xii) Economics, Sociology and Trade Unionism; (xiii) Economics, Commerce and Marketing; (xiv) Economics, Commerce and Home Economics.

The new combination of courses in Arts and Sciences requires an inter-disciplinary approach to knowledge and teaching methods. The belief that exposure of students to inter-disciplinary teaching methods in order to make them aware of the needs and problems of the community, and to sensitize them to the social reality is gaining currency.

The introduction of action programmes through vocationalization of courses at the Degree level will mean that both the teachers and the students will move out of the sacred precincts of the colleges and the universities and go to the community, identify themselves with people and their problems, jointly explore the area of their work on an inter-disciplinary basis, gain experience through work projects and simultaneously allow the community also to receive benefits of their knowledge and experience. This process not only makes teaching purposeful and meaningful, but sensitizes the members of the university community, who are a privileged group, to contribute their mite to the good of the society.

6. PSYCHOLOGICAL TESTING FOR MAKING HIGHER EDUCATION EFFECTIVE

One of the major goals of higher education is to facilitate the physical, social and psychological development of individual students. This is done mainly through health services, co-curricular services and psychological services extended to students. Testing, like counselling, forms a principal aspect of psychological services.

Psychological tests can be powerful tools for assisting students in making educational, vocational and personal adjustment. Well-constructed and adequately standardized tests can provide estimates of a student's achievement in various academic areas, his potential for future educational development, his pattern of educational and vocational interests, his attitudes and his emotional structure. Knowledge of these factors can be extremely useful in helping to identify a student's problem in the course of counselling and in suggesting possible alternative solutions to his problem. Thus, psychological testing goes a long way in solving various problems faced in the field of higher education.

Testing is useful in the selection of students for admission to institutions of higher education. At present, students are admitted mainly on the basis of their achievement in their last examinations. And their achievement in the examinations depends not only on their academic ability but also upon the kind of instruction they received in the institution they last attended. Thus, a highly capable student who happened to attend a mediocre or poor secondary school is placed at a marked disadvantage on such an achievement test. The use of a well-standardized test of scholastic aptitude, which places less emphasis on accumulated information and more emphasis on the student's ability to reason with facts that are given to him, might well help in identifying those students who have a high potential for further study but who have had a poor educational background.

Testing is also useful in regard to students who although generally admissible to the institution, have some specific educational handicap which might interfere with their progress. Many Indian students encounter difficulties in their college work either because they may have a reading handicap or because they may be suffering from some emotional difficulty, or for any of variety of education-retarding causes. A well-developed classification testing programme could identify such capable, but handicapped students before they were enrolled in classes where they are likely to encounter difficulties. Once such students are identified, it would be possible to establish remedial or therapeutic programmes which could aid them in overcoming their handicaps, and thus make them better able to take full advantage of the educational opportunities offered by the institutions.

Psychological testing is useful not only in selecting students properly, and in overcoming their handicaps if they have any, but also in improving their instruction. Well-devised diagnostic achievement tests administered at the beginning of a course can provide an instructor with information about the level of attainment of his students before he starts teaching. Such tests can tell him which areas of his course need to be stressed and which areas have already been fairly well mastered by his students. This sort of information would make it possible for the instructor to reorganize his class sections so that each section represents a more homogeneous group in regard to attainment of proficiency in his subject. Then he could plan his instruction in such a way as to meet the special needs of each group.

Though psychological testing thus proves to be useful in making educational system effective, it is unfortunate that very few instructors are trained in psychometrics, with the result that their testing procedures are more often than not naive and even self-defeating. To remedy this state of affairs university psychology departments could be requisitioned to offer test consultation services on a voluntary basis for instructors who need assistance in the construction, administration, scoring and interpretation of tests. Collaboration between the instructional staff and the psychometrically sophisticated members of the psychology discipline could produce test instruments which are at once valid and reliable.

7. ENTRANCE TESTS AT THE UNIVERSITIES

The universities are now going ahead with their programme of conducting entrance tests for admission into various post-graduate courses. The public has already raised a hue and cry. Where is the need for an entrance test, they ask, when the candidates seeking admission into the post-graduate courses are no other than the very graduates the same universities have produced? Why not the universities go by the marks they themselves have awarded, ask some others, and select the candidates strictly on the basis of merit? Is it not tantamount to distrusting the marks the universities themselves have awarded?, some others put it bluntly.

The detractors of the Entrance Test system do not stop there. They argue that the Entrance Tests business will create many problems in the academic world. The process of taking students through an Entrance Test will give a lot of scope for manipulation at various levels so as to push in the candidates backed by influential sources. They feel that this will result in the forfeiture of seats by some of the really deserving.

The main targets of attack will be Heads of departments in the universities who will be entrusted with the responsibilities of setting the question papers, conducting the entrance test and evaluating the answer scripts in the disciplines concerned. The Indian conditions being what they are, the Heads of departments may be subjected to various pressures and the honest among them need a lot of moral courage to stem the tide.

There is another possibility too for mischief. Even if the Entrance Tests are conducted properly and the students are selected without any prejudice, favouritism and malpractice, there may be a few mischievous elements among those not selected who will concoct and kick a row and even instigate the other unselected students to go on strike or gherao the Head of the department concerned, the Principal or the Vice-Chancellor.

While all this is not ruled out, a case for Entrance Tests for admission into post-graduate courses in the universities can still be made out. First of all, there is no reason why the universities should not be allowed to exercise their right to select the candidates they need according to their own norms and methods, of course, by taking every care to see that the method is made foolproof. Why not the universities enjoy the right the professional institutions of Engineering and Medicine have been enjoying all along, with a view to selecting the right students with high competence.

It is true that the candidates seeking admission into the universities have been produced by the same universities. But, it should be noted that the B.A., B.Sc. and B.Com. are not preparatory courses for M.A., M.Sc. and M.Com., but entities in themselves. A student who secured very high marks at the undergraduate level, often through cramming, need not necessarily have the aptitude and competence for the pursuit of his subject at the post-graduate level. On the other hand, a student who happened to score low at the undergraduate level for various reasons may have the necessary aptitude and potentialities for the pursuit of his subject at the post-graduate level.

Hence, the need to design the Entrance Tests in such a way as to find out whether or not the candidate in question possesses the necessary aptitude and, what is more, the inherent potentialities for the study of the chosen subject at the post-graduate level.

More often than not, the Entrance Tests are conducted to scan the knowledge of the candidate in the chosen field. This is not desirable here inasmuch as the candidate's knowledge of the subject has already been tested at the undergraduate level. There is no point in trying to test his proven knowledge again. It will be nothing but redundancy and sheer waste of time and energy.

8. VICE-CHANCELLOR AS EDUCATIONAL LEADER

The current strategies to combat campus disruptions such as closing the colleges indefinitely and making the students vacate the hostels, or calling the police to the campus to suppress any eruption of student indicipline tend to provoke the very atmosphere and behaviour by which campus disorders are precipitated. If, on the other hand, a sense of shared purposes or meaningful relationships is maintained, such threats of disorder as do occur can be dealt with more easily. Calling the police to the campus should be considered only as the last, desperate resort. For, it is never a sign of strength on the part of educational administrators, nor a basis for hope that the institution's problems will finally be resolved.

A final essential feature of effective educational leadership of a Vice-Chancellor is his recognition of the fact that the university cannot creatively and meaningfully perform its activities without proper interaction between it and the community around. The Vice-Chancellor must make every effort to explain the problems of his university to the general public and to interpret the latter's concerns to students and faculty. For this purpose, members of the campus must be encouraged to meet groups in the community and interested citizens could be invited to the campus. Thus, the Vice-Chancellor has to work constantly at improved campus-community relations.

The job of running a university is generally seen primarily in terms of the concept of administration. Administration is understood as essentially a matter of organisational management. And the university Vice-Chancellor is perceived as the organisational chief executive, responsible for seeing that the managerial operations are properly carried out.

But, these conventional notions of academic governance no longer adequately describe the relative urgency, difficulties or demands of the actual functions of a Vice-Chancellor. While the organisational tasks remain as essential as ever, the overriding dimension of academic governance today is no longer a matter of mere administrative management but of effective educational leadership. The critical skill required is not so much managerial as educational. And, the acid test for Vice-Chancellors is no longer simply the quality of their administrative performance, but their effectiveness as educational leaders.

The career of the Vice-Chancellor who undertakes such educational leadership will, of course, be precarious. Since his function is to overcome, rather than avoid the current polarities in regard to higher education, he must, of necessity, expose himself at every turn. To be capable of this by being equal to the task, the Vice-Chancellor must be secure in his personality and be able to consider himself expendable in his position.

He must derive his highest satisfaction not from his official title, but from what it may enable him to contribute to the vital, educational and cultural processes in which his institution is engaged.

We urgently need such humanistic, effective and involved educational leadership to facilitate the continuing renewal of our academic enterprise. And, we need it to protect higher education from the distortive inroads, being attempted against its essential principles from both on campus and off.

V

NEW ROLE OF TEACHERS

1. CRISIS IN UNIVERSITY TEACHING

In the last ten years, the Indian universities have been progressing by accumulating crises — the crisis of numbers, the crisis of finance, the crisis of political interference, and the crisis of student unrest. To this disturbing list of crises one is constrained to add the crisis of teaching.

Though universities are primarily teaching institutions, research is obviously getting the better of teaching. In other words, teaching is tending to become the servant of scholarship and research, instead of being at least its equal. And, more often than not, research is concentrated on at the cost of teaching. This is what makes the crisis in teaching in our universities today.

Many members of university staff do not seem to give enough of their best and freshest attention to post-graduate teaching. They are more interested in their own research work and in supervision of research scholars. Thus, though they are primarily teachers, their concentration is on publication of papers and books and production of M. Phils and Ph. Ds.

Perhaps, the university teachers cannot be blamed for this paradoxical phenomenon. The very system of university staffing and of promotions to higher cadres is such that the teachers are made, rather tempted, to indulge in research and publication activities even at the cost of their teaching.

Today, a wise university teacher is he who spends most of his time and energy on publication of research papers and books rather than on teaching his students. For, no university is bothered about taking into consideration what kind of teacher one is, at the time of interviewing the candidate for promotion to a higher cadre. "How many papers have you published and how many books? How many doctorates have you produced and how many candidates are you guiding for M. Phil. and Ph. D.?" — these are the questions invariably put to the promotion-seeking university teachers at every interview in almost every university.

Small wonder, therefore, if research has become an honorific word in Indian universities. And, many of those who glorify it know more about research than they know about teaching. It is generally said, and believed too, that one cannot be a good university teacher unless one carries along with his teaching a substantial commitment to research, and that one cannot keep alive in one's subject unless one is at work on the ever-widening frontiers of knowledge.

But, it is erroneous to think that one cannot be a good university teacher unless one is a dedicated researcher. One who is temperamentally suited to, and has a flair for, teaching, and, what is more, capable of strong commitment to teaching, could be good and successful teacher. One need not necessarily be an able researcher in order to be a good university teacher. Also, not all able researchers can hold their passion for research and their duties to post-graduate and undergraduate teaching in the delicate balance that is called for. Moreover, it cannot be denied that some very able researchers are indifferent, and even dreary, teachers.

No one can be a good teacher unless he is vigorously alive in his subject. If his subject does not have a surge of excitement for him, it certainly will not have for his students. Once he has that deep and innate interest in his subject, he will not lack excitement in broadening his grasp of his subject, absorbing and digesting the new knowledge that is being won on the frontier. He could also instil in his students a lot of curiosity in the innumerable links his subject has with other cognate subjects, and in the illumination that his subject throws on the whole human enterprise.

Taken in this way, a subject that is worth teaching bristles with pedagogical problems — how to organize it so that its complexities yield to student effort, how to improve lucidity in exposition with the right words and the telling illustrations, how to design suitable topics enabling the good student to march with him to the heights. Is there not here enough intellectual activity, enough bait to keep curiosity alive, enough demand on a scholarly mind to last a life-time?

Research should, no doubt, find its proper place in the Indian universities. The purpose of research must be to enhance the quality of teaching as well as to enliven it. In short, research shouled make university teacher a better teacher. But, in practice, research and teaching seem to be going on two parallel lines. This is uncalled for. Besides having application and relevance to the felt needs of society, research should be a handmaid to teaching.

Anyway, it is time the present undue concentration on research work in universities, even at the cost of teaching, was modified and post-graduate teaching restored to parity. This could possibly be done only when the university authorities give as much importance to the quality of the candidate's teaching as to his capacity for research, in recruiting and promoting university teachers. The university must work out modalities to assess the quality of teaching of its teachers. In assessing the teachers, the universities would do well in involving the students also by way of administering questionnaires on the performance of teachers. The sooner this is done the better for the university life.

2. TEACHERS AS INTERPRETERS AND MEDIATORS

With explosion of knowledge, on the one hand, and explosion of aspirations of students, on the other, the problems of higher education have acquired greater complexity and magnitude. Knowledge is developing so rapidly that at any given moment, available knowledge may already be becoming obsolete. On top of that, students expect more from their teachers now than they did in earlier days.

Therefore, the role of the teacher as the dispenser of knowledge does not seem to be very relevant now. It is more important for him to initiate his students into the art of learning by way of helping them acquire the right mental attitudes and learning habits. Thus, the teacher's role is changing. His authoritative delivery of knowledge is being supplemented by his spending more time diagnosing the learner's needs, motivating and encouraging study, and checking the knowledge acquired.

The teacher is now expected not only to inculcate knowledge but also to encourage thinking. He has to become more an adviser, a partner to talk to. He has to help seek out conflicting arguments rather than hand out ready-made truths. For this he will have to devote more and more time and energy to productive and creative activities.

At the UNESCO conference in Geneva in 1975, member states identified in the role of teachers the following general trends of change towards :

(a) a shift in emphasis from transmission of knowledge to organization of the student learning, with maximum use of new resources of learning in the community;

(b) individualization of learning and changed structure in teacher-student relationships; and

(c) the necessity to work more closely with parents and other people in the community.

Naturally, becoming a successful teacher presents a greater challenge today than at any previous time in history. As an interpreter, the teacher has to place new knowledge and new experience within the context of what is already known and understood by the students. In order to be a good mediator, he has to understand a great deal about the nature of knowledge and also about the way in which people at various ages and stages of development perceive the world around them. As a guide, he has to teach the student 'how to learn' rather than stuff his mind with factual information.

Then, teachers are being challenged to utilise new approaches and methods in an effort to improve learning results. They have to seek improved ways of teaching by developing new programmes and instructional strategies such as enquiry approaches, simulation games, contract approaches, computer-assisted instruction and programmed learning materials. What is more, the teacher is confronted perpetually with the problem of determining his role as a consumer of the past and as an innovator of the future.

To meet the new challenges boldly and to play his role meaningfully, the teacher, besides imparting knowledge, has to help the young students to understand the components of their conscious and unconscious personalities, the meaning of their dreams and aspirations and the nature of their relations with one another and with community at large. In short, he has to teach his students not only the art of learning but also the art of living and working in a society which they must create as an embodiment of their cherished ideals and realized goals.

3. NEW DIRECTIONS IN THE ROLE OF TEACHERS

Though a thorough mastery of the subject is indispensable, it can no longer be said to constitute the sole measure of a teacher's qualifications, for adequate guidance through teaching involves more than an undertaking of curriculum materials. It is very essential for the teacher to have familiarity with the characteristics of students and the society to which they belong.

If education is to be highly effective in the modification of pupil behaviour along desired lines, no intelligent approach can be made except on the basis of thorough familiarity with the basic conditions which determine the behaviour of an individual as such or as a member of social group. Therefore, to be really capable of exercising a guiding influence over students, a teacher must have lived life himself, must understand the social and biological drives of adolescence and, what is more, to be able to utilize these forces in the development of a classroom curriculum based upon the needs and interests of youth in the modern age.

The teacher should also be conversant with the processes through which experiences lead to modifications of behaviour. As an educational psychologist puts it, "to be educative, an experience must utilize past experience, must involve familiar behaviour, but, in addition, must lead on to more advanced or complex behaviour". So, unless there is a perceptible change in emotional reaction, pattern of thinking, interest, or in some other sphere of a person's actual behaviour, an experience cannot be said to be educative. Hence, the teacher must keep in mind while teaching not only the goals toward which pupils are being guided, but processes by which personal, experiential growth takes place. Personal growth rather than achieving superiority over others is the new emphasis in education today.

Secondly, the teacher should be familiar with the characteristics of the present-day society as well as with the various societal types represented in his classes. He should be aware of the changes occurring in a pupil's social environment, and also understand the particular problems involved in belonging to different groups, the conflicts and bonds existing among their members, the methods of co-ordination, integration, and co-operation by virtue of which individuals from various societal levels and types manage to coexist. Taking cognizance of alternative values and of the need for re-examining present institutions in the light of changing conditions equips the student with the ability to participate in effecting the necessary behavioural modifications.

The student could be said to have been really educated only when he is in a position to adjust himself to his society, share in its experiences and contribute to its maintenance. This demands on the part of the student an understanding of the aims and interests of the social group, together with a sensitivity to its changing needs, a desire to cooperate by granting the rights of others, a readiness to share the obligations as well as the rights and privileges of membership in the group, and vocational preparation to contribute to social welfare by rendering the best service of which one is capable and by virtue of which he can maintain himself. The teacher must be able to detect the special capabilities of each student and to devise learning situations whereby the student fully develops these qualities that will enable him to take his rightful place as a responsible and well-integrated member of the society he lives in.

4. TOWARDS REVAMPING HISTORY TEACHING

A close and objective look at the teaching of history today in our schools and colleges calls for a drastic need of revision and change. Even after fifty years of Independence, we are teaching British history conventionally without realizing that the history of Europe is not less important and that the history of the Middle East and South-East Asia is, from some points of view, more important. What is worse, the British history is being taught to students with little background in the history of Britain. In other words, we are teaching an effete curriculum in history by methods so dated that it hardly fits into the New Education Policy of India.

The history texts used in the classroom reiterate the hard and sometimes dull fact. They do not portray memorable struggles of sovereignity in terms of personality or ideas. For instance, they do not attempt to relate history in Britain to history in India or other parts of the world. No effort is made to open the doors of historical fiction to Indian students. No attempt is made to dramatise significant and spectacular events of history. The entire procession of history passes into a drab textbook, eras strung together with dates. As a result, the students get bogged down in cold dates and places of the past, rather than comprehending the present in the light of the human experience of the past.

Let alone British history, even Indian history is not taught properly. We are teaching Indian history with a panoramic sweep that suggests that our students can digest history with greater ease and speed than any other students in the world. The Guptas, the Mughals, the Afghans, the Marathas, the Cholas, the Pallavas and the Sathavahanas are all alike consigned to the museum of the past in which what was and is most living in the ideas of men remains most dead for their children. No comparisons are instituted, no study made of the brevity of empires, of their sustained and common tendencies to fall apart, of the difficulties in delegating power and the constant problems in governing a sub-continent of India's size and complexity that persist down to our own times.

The first essential in teaching history is to go back to the roots of history, and there is no root more penetrating than the geography of the country concerned. While teaching the history of India, let us, therefore, turn to immediate geography of India with its unique diversity and astounding range. Let us empty the classrooms now and then and turn the students into the open, away from the date-line, the textbook, the blackboard, the dreary maps and the drone of uninspired teaching. We should not, however, turn them as most people do upon national monuments or museums, as this is a second-rate way of teaching history. The monument is a historical result : it is not a cuase of history. The museum is an assemblage of things that does not necesarily reflect the thinking of an age, unless these things are superlatively well organized. Unfortunately, our museums are not yet so well organized.

If we are to revolutionize the teaching of history in our schools and colleges, it must be through sheer joy. For only a joy in education will lead our students to rediscover their country in the Nehruvian sense. The Youth Hostel Movement that has started in India, but has as yet made little headway, can use the clarion cry to "Discover India" to stimulate this process. Schools and colleges must organize regular visits to historical sites and, in a drive to teach, take the students over the length and breadth of the country with a view to forcing it to yield its historical secrets. What it looks like, what it is like, what it yields, — all this the student, who travels throughout India, will learn to know. Automatically the basic lesson of history is taught and learnt.

Once we open up the countryside, the rest will be the story of discovery that is the reward of good teachers. On his own initiative the student will open the creaking doors of the college library. He will read historical fiction that will round off the story of his country.

Yet another way of revolutionizing history teaching is to dramatize history as a regular part of teaching. Instead of the pathetic school or college day drama meant for sheer entertainment, we can teach history through regular drama. We can commission one-act plays on Indian history and teach the students to produce them. This will drive them into the study of art and cosume history. And the doors of the past will swing slowly open through the irresitible media of clothes, customs, manners and idiom. For instance, we can produce a panoramic pageant of ballet, music and drama to tell the story of the Gandhian era. Discussion on it could be conducted in the classroom. The children would learn that Gandhian history has provided them with targets for today, the historic point of which they had so consistently missed in the classroom. What is more, they would begin to understand the authentic business of history.

In teaching history what we have to make clear to the student is that the business of history is not to make us comfortable but uncomfortable. What we have to impress upon them is that the business of history is to destroy complacency, to stimulate discontent and "to draw the human soul into uneasy life when it is in danger of achieving easy death." It shall be the business of history to restore to the spirit of man that symbol of a soaring destiny that fired the Elizabethans of the European Renaissance, and led Columbus through mutiny and peril to a new world that he fell upon and kissed with the passion in discovery.

VI

MULTIFACETED ROLE OF UNIVERSITY LIBRARIES

1. RANGANATHAN : THE FATHER OF LIBRARY SCIENCE IN INDIA

The quality of library services in any country is determined by the quality of practitioners in library and information science available in that country. Though classified as a developing country, India is one of the most advanced countries when education for librarianship is considered. For this, the entire credit goes to the late Ranganathan whose Birth Centenary was observed all over the country. He ventured into what was an unexplored territory in India — the field of education for librarianship. Apart from transforming the university and college libraries in India, he laid the foundation for library education in the institutions of higher learning. He brought about revolutionary changes in the regular, routine functions of libraries by way of systematising them and introducing many management techniques which was not done earlier in Indian situation. Above all, he was the guiding force in library movement in most of the States in India. Small wonder, therefore, if Ranganathan is considered the Father of Library Science in India.

Ranganathan was born on August 12th, 1892, at Shiyali in the Tanjavoor District of Tamil Nadu to Seethalakshmi and Ramamritha Iyer as their first child. As a student he had quick understanding, grasp and good memory. After M.A. in Mathematics, he started his career in Madras University. He was appointed the first Librarian of Madras University in 1924 and worked there for the next 20 years. It was a turning point in the history of the Library Movement in India. He was sent to England on deputation for training in Library Science. He did his apprenticeship in Croydon Public Libraries under the famous Librarian, W.C. Brwick Sayers, and others. After returning from England with a rich experience, Ranganathan founded the Madras Library Association in 1928. He was the first in India to start the school of Library Science in 1929. He turned his interest to library legislation and drafted the Model Library Act in 1930 and the first Library Bill for Bengal State in 1931. Furthermore, he drafted the constitution of the Indian Library Association which was started in 1933.

Ranganathan's distinguished work in the library profession attracted Sir Maurice Gwyer, the Chief Justice of India and the Vice-Chancellor of the University of Delhi, who invited him for working in Delhi University. He established the Department of Library Science for running B. Lib. Sc., and M. Lib. Sc., courses and also provided facility for Ph.D. in Library Science by research in 1948.

Ranganathan visited Europe and U.S.A. from June to September, 1948, delivered lectures on library education at different libraries and taught library science in various universities. He attended the conference of Federation of International Standards Organization as well as the Conference of the International Standards Organization Technical Committee at the Hague in July, 1948. With the collaboration of UNESCO he helped to establish INSDOC (Indian National Scientific Documentation Centre) in 1952.

Ranganathan's work and reputation spread far and wide and his advice and guidance were sought after by various types of library organizations all over the world. He was elected Vice-President of the International Federation of Documentation during 1953-56 and 1959-61. He was also elected Honorary Vice-President of the Library Association of the United Kingdom. In 1958, he visited United States, Canada and Japan where he was visiting professor in various universities. He was the first Chairman of the Library Committee of the University Grants Commission (UGC) and played a key role in the development of university and college libraries in the country. And, as the Chairman of the Library Committee of the Indian Standards Institutions, he developed a number of standards relating to classification, cataloguing, library buildings, fittings and furniture as guidelines for the development and progress of libraries in India. Until the end of his life, to the very last day, Ranganathan kept on working. He died on 27th September, 1972 after 80 fruitful years of his life.

Ranganathan was a man of rare ability, great talent and erudite scholarship. In 1931, he published his world famous *Five Laws of Library Science* which made a deep impact on many aspects of librarianship. The well known Five Laws are :

1. Books are for use;
2. Every Reader his/her book;
3. Every book its reader;
4. Save the time of the reader; and
5. Library is a growing organization.

Ranganathan's "Five Laws" are the fundamental normative principles of Library Science. As Mohindar Singh, an Indian Librarian, puts it, "Like Newton's three Laws of Motion, Ranganathan's Five Laws brought a revolution in the thinking of the Library world." Whereas the first law revolutionaized the outlook of the libraries, the second and third laws made that revolution as thorough as possible. The fifth law fits very well in the modern librarianship and reference services of a library. They furnish an interpretative explanation of the empirical facts of experience and of the technology found necessary in experience in relation to library services.

Thus, Ranganathan's Five Laws essentially constitute a fundamental contribution to the development of library science, documentation and information service. Library science has attained the status of a full-fledged social science with reference to these fundamental normative principles. They serve as the basis for *a priori* research in library science helping the derivation of deduced principles. In this sense, they constitute the most significant contribution to the development of library science as a recognized social science. They are relevant in regard to library science in the past, at present, and in the future. That is, perhaps, why they are universally accepted as the library philosophy in India and abroad.

Ranganathan was *par excellence* an innovator and an original thinker. The application of scientific management to libraries at present owes its origin to the ideas generated by Ranganathan. His ideas on functional planning, job analysis, time scheme and librametry are the bases on which modern management techniques like system planning, input-output analysis, work analysis techniques, MBO, participative management, time series analysis, cost-effectiveness models and statistical techniques found applications in library and information services.

Also, Ranganathan brought innovative changes in designing new systems like Three Card System and modification over charging system and finding specifications to suit Indian libraries. Again, he devised library staff formula which is still followed as a standard. With the constraints of limited funds, physical facilities and resources in Indian libraries, he had suggested a good number of innovative steps like optimum use of document resources.

As a leader of the library movement, Ranganathan encouraged the use of computers in libraries and predicted that reference libraries will have to act as programmers and do bibliographic on-line searching for users soon. He was quite right in his prediction because computers have invaded the field of library and information science, especially in the Western world and many reference librarians are doing computer searching for the users. The computer usage is on the increase not only by reference librarians but by other librarians who are engaged in cataloguing, acquisition, circulation and inter-library loan system.

To conclude, Ranganathan turned librarianship into a wanted profession by the dint of his sincere efforts and effective leadership. In his life time of work, he showed us the way, but now we must collectively do what one man tried to do single-handed. It is our responsibility to carry on the work done by him, especially in the field of reference service which is the key to all other services. For, according to him, the essence of librarianship is reference service which is the preponderant achievement of modern humanism in library science. Therefore, all libraries should make this important service as their top priority. All libraries should have well trained librarians to serve the needs of their users for all hours the library is open. They should select the best and most recent updated reference books for the reference collection and what is more, keep themselves abreast of the modern trends of reference as well as other services of librarianship including on-line bibliographic service and on-line catalogue. We should ensure that the use of reference tools and awareness of reference service are as fundamentally a part of education as the 3 R's and should be introduced from the earliest years of a child's education.

2. MODERN UNIVERSITY LIBRARY AS A MULTIFACETED LEARNING CENTRES

Libraries are no longer, as Socrates would have us believe, shrines for worship, but delivery rooms for the birth of new ideas. The library is central to the responsibilities of a university and to the functions of a college at all levels of learning. Higher education depends critically on acquiring the knowhow for using a modern library to the best advantage. Highlighting the cardinal role of a library, different Commissions on higher education have called it by impressive terms, such as 'the heart of the university', 'fulcrum of university education', 'the workshop of the scholars' and 'the laboratory of the learned'. Modern educationists would aptly call libraries intellectual workshops.

As Paul Buck, an eminent Harvard University Librarian remarked, "a good collection of books attracts a good faculty, and a good faculty, in turn, attracts good students." Thus, the reputation of a university depends on the status of its library. Hence, the need for the libraries to function as intellectual workshops rather than as museums of books.

Higher education requires the assimilation of vast amounts of knowledge and its further development. Classroom teaching can only serve a small part of the requirement since it can only give the students an outline of what they need to know. The students need the availability of a large volume of material to form their own judgement. Faculties need material to pursue research and teaching. Higher education requires keeping up-to-date in one's own field and research in new ways of presentation of material.

Small wonder, therefore, if the importance of library in university education in India has been duly emphasised by educationist, librarians, scholars, education commissions and committees. The National Education Policy of 1986 highlighted the role of libraries in supporting higher education and gave it a new orientation. A review of the statistical position reveals that remarkable progress has been made during the past four decades in establishing new libraries and strengthening the old ones. The addition of books and journals now enables a library to meet the needs of a larger student population.

In 1927, we had only 15 University libraries for a total student population of 91,000, each catering to the needs of approximately 6,000 readers. By the year 1951, we had 28 University libraries for about 1,86,650 students, each taking care of about 6,670 students on an average. In 1985, the number of University libraries rose to 155 to serve the needs of 32,00,000 students, thus raising the average number of users of a single library to 20,645. At the current rate, we will have about 200 libraries to serve a student population of some 80,00,000 by turn of the century, which would mean an average number of 40,000 for each library.

The quantitative expansion of libraries resulting in the increased number of users is heartening, but the qualitative aspect has not been given proper attention, thereby leading to a decline in the standard of library services. The finest task before the present generation of librarians is, therefore, to educate the reader in the intellectual use of the library. A developing country like India with sparse resources needs to educate millions of its library users in conceptualizing their information needs and matching them with the resources of the library by comprehending the methodology of the library. The best user has to be his own librarian.

The librarian can discharge his obligation only by shaping the library users into self-directed learners. To do this, he has to introduce the learner to the world of exploration. He has to initiate him in the processes of such exploration both personal and participative. He has also to inspire him to undertake arduous tasks for the purpose. Above all, he should help him to chart the course of action and to make the breakthroughs on his way. In this journey of the student for knowledge, the library, its resources, its personnel, its modalities of work, its climate and culture, and its various services have to provide him support which will prove critically vital in sustaining his morale, his patience, his commitment and his will to learn on his own. Such tactical support will reinforce his faith in himself and in his ability to pursue his goals of learning.

The most important feature of modern times, influencing development and international competition, is that the rate of growth of information and knowledge is faster than ever before and is still accelerating. The world famous futurist, Alvin Toffler, calls the 21st century space age, computer age, information age or electronics era. Blaise Cronin describes the future society as 'Information Society' and predicts the emergence of information workers. These developments are the impact of the phenomenon known as 'Information Explosion'. The fast pace of information generation in geometrical progression has ushered in a challenging situation for the scientists and researchers.

Nowadays, the problem is not the scarcity of information. Rather, it is excessive information. In most fields, abstracts of publications, especially of the latest research articles, are available but even these have become so numerous that abstracts of the various abstracting services are becoming necessary. The aim of libraries, therefore, will not be to have upto date information, but up-to-the-minute information. We have to accept the challenge to assist in making of a better informed world, a safer and happier place to live in. A growing role for the library would lie in information, counselling and individual training, advising the users on services and products appropriate to their needs, and how best to use them.

The library of a modern university is, therefore, conceived of as a multi-faceted learning centre dedicated to serve the multi-function agenda of the university as being operated by its students, teachers, scholars, researchers and knowledge workers. To play this role effectively, the modern university or college library should have learning resources of a large variety to be acquired, maintained and replenished under a far-sighted policy. Above all, it should have a wider gamut of library services offered through imaginative, pro-learning management practices, and a team of personnel dedicated to the cause of education of young men and women who are accountable to themselves and the community at large.

Libraries with distinct structural identities and facilities become the hub of student's activities. Libraries should be well housed and well used. However, mere buildings do not make good libraries. To equip them with books that can be preserved for posterity is a task as Herculean as finding resources for building it. With accent on novel methods of information storage, processing and retrieval, libraries in future bid fair to rise to the occasion in information societies. Thanks to the UGC, the colleges are getting equipped with xerox machines and reprographic gadgets. The computer facility is also planned to explore the possibility of the optimum utilisation of the available resources. The challenges of the future demand that the students are adept in communication skills, reading and writing skills, and skills for acquiring and using information available in libraries.

We can create a congenial atmosphere for promotion of research activities in universities only when their libraries acquire materials in anticipation and, of course, on demand. We are in an age of specialisation, witnessing the emergence of specialities and super-specialities in various fields. University libraries need to equip themselves to meet the challenging task by building up the widest possible collection in specific interest areas or specialisations. The collection has to fulfil the futuristic requirements in the emerging and potential fields of significance, and not just providing material in areas of immediate concern. The pattern and content of collection of books and other reference material really reflect the quality standards of libraries.

To conclude, a modern university library, as multifaceted learning centre, has to perform a package of many related services — provision of books, journals, documentation, selective dissemination of information, current awareness, indexing and abstracting, bibliography, reprography, translation, inter-library loan, referral service, advisory service on source materials, and retrieval of information and documents. Research studies need to be conducted from time to time to improve library services. Thus, a university library has to play a vibrant role of an intellectual workshop for cross-fertilization of ideas and for serving as a centre for perpetuating and extending the horizons of knowledge.

3. LIBRARIES AS MEDIA OF MASS EDUCATION

The traditional meaning of library is a 'collection of books for reading'. And libraries have been popularly known as 'storehouses of knowledge' and 'treasures of wisdom'. They have been urban-oriented and have predominantly become a component of educational institutes. The universities have fairly good libraries thanks to the generous grants of the U.G.C., but then, they are accessible and useful only to students, research scholars and teachers. The college libraries have become museums, and are not properly made use of even by teachers and students. As a result, dust gathers on books and they gradually become food for white ants. There are public libraries too in cities and big towns serving more as reading rooms for those who cannot afford to purchase newspapers and magazines. Thus, the libraries are serving only the educated at present.

But, in a country like India where we have nearly 50% of illiterates mainly residing in villages, one may question the traditional role of urban-oriented libraries. Since the majority of India's population is illiterate, the traditional libraries have very limited use. A new dimension has, therefore, to be added in the present context, whereby the library would now be a centre for disseminating knowledge not only through reading material but also through other media of communication.

We have learnt by our endless experimentation and long experience that our country's educational problems can never be solved with a purely institutional approach. We now have 100 million children in 6 lakhs of institutions. If all the children between the ages of 5 and 14 are to be enrolled in schools, as our Constitution demands, we would need at least one million institutions right now. And with our population growing at the rate of 2.2% per year, we shall reach a total of about one billion by the end of this century and then we would need to provide schools for about 300 million children. For one thing, there just is not enough money to build and equip the millions of schools that would be required. Hence, the active exploration of mass education through mass media like radio, television, films and Adult Education.

One of the least explored media of mass education is library. With the present emphasis of the Government of India on Adult Education, Continuing Education, Functional Education and Literacy drive, libraries could play a vital role by becoming the centres where such activities take place meaningfully. The current glaring communication gap between the urban and rural communities, between the educated and illiterate population can be bridged by way of making the present libraries also become the major instrument in mass education.

It is, therefore, necessary that a new meaning and dimension is given to formation of libraries if the intention is to generate continuous learning process. Then, the functioning of the libraries will have to change in this context and more meaningful and relevant methods of communication will have to be incorporated so that libraries can become centres for Continuing Education, using non-formal strategies of communicating new ideas and knowledge to cover all units of the population.

Thus, the library could serve as a mass media for learning and mutual understanding. As media of mass education, the library would be linked with motivation for achievement, self-awareness and actual development. This would result in the process of social change to improve the quality of life. In other words, the functioning of the library and dissemination of knowledge should centre round the desired 'social change' and development.

To play this new role successfully, the library should consist of not only reading material in the form of books and journals but also various types of communication systems — posters, pictures, sketches, photographs, charts, flash cards, motion pictures and film strips on health, agriculture, and animal husbandry. As part of its functions, the library should also arrange dramas, skits, lectures and discussions, Festival of Ideas and other programmes such as celebration of Human Rights Day.

In its new role, the library becomes a centre for developing communication and teaching aids for better learning and understanding and for widening the horizon of the community by making information available on subjects of rural interest. The process would be of continuous education and we should keep in mind the different groups — illiterates, neo-literates, women, children, and functional groups like farmers and weavers — to cater to their needs and development.

4. PUBLIC LIBRARY AS PEOPLE'S UNIVERSITY

Library is *par excellence* a social institution. Born in civilised literate society, it grows and develops in response to social conditions and needs for equipping the people with the necessary proportion of accumulated knowledge and preparing them for cooperative life. And advancement of civilisation requires that each member of society shall acquire general knowledge in proportion to the demands of his cooperative life. Further, each generation must take active possession of every part of the accumulated learning that has a utilitarian and human value, in order to contribute positively to the welfare of society.

Under modern conditions this store of knowledge has become so vast that no single individual can grasp it all. Hence, the enormous significance of the library which has been created by actual necessities in modern civilisation and which has become a necessary unit in the social fabric. Today the library is the chief instrument for accumulating and disseminating man's intellectual heritage. The library has become an effective institution for organised self-education.

Libraries, in general, and public libraries, in particular, have a very significant role to play in the development of the social, cultural and educational life of modern man, especially in a country like India where all are not in a position to receive the benefit of formal education. Hence, the dire need for library service to all the classes of people, particularly to those who are not able to prosecute their studies further and reap the fruits of university education. Library service is a special necessity for the steady development of any human being. A local library is, therefore, the social nerve centre of the community.

The traditional conception of public library has thus undergone a tremendous change from the early notion of 'museum of books', to the present idea of a 'people's university'. The public library is a product of modern democracy and a practical demonstration of modern man's faith in universal education as a life-long process. It aims at making books and journals available to all by an efficient library service and an integrated system of libraries. It is geared to the daily life and habits of the people. It seeks to do its best to the community, drawing people of all ages to it and inviting them to make the most profitable use of it for information, scholarship, research and recreation. It helps one and all to educate themselves continuously, irrespective of class, creed, caste or sex, to be responsible citizens with capacity for independent thinking and to share common culture for co-operative living.

Modern democracy which is based on adult franchise depends for its success on universal mass education. No real democracy can be established until there are well-educated people. And no institution can play a better and greater role than a public library in achieving this end. For, the goal of modern public libraries is the democratic ideal of equal opportunity for all to get knowledge. Not all in a society are in a position to receive formal schooling for education. The public library becomes a place for learning for such unfortunate people. Kept open for 12 to 14 hours a days the public library welcomes the common man and gives him an opportunity to develop himself according to his desire, capacity and need. It is in this sense that a good and well-developed public library becomes a people's university.

The public library is an instrument for raising the cultural standards and effecting an all-round progress of its users. By changing and increasing the reading habits and tastes of the people, it helps to raise the level of culture. As a cultural and intellectual centre, the public library covers all stages of thirst for knowledge, from the incipient curiosity to the intellectual quest.

The library is a potent force capable of building a better society by its vitality, variety, quality and extent of its service. It is a necessary complement to all educational services. As a social institution, its function is not only to satisfy the need for books but also to promote the desire for learning.

Besides being a supplement to formal schooling, the public library can, in a large measure, fill in the gaps of knowledge and awareness of those people whose education and training have necessarily been of a specialised nature. It is actually helping millions of citizens to move forward in vocational and professional skills, in family living, in the pleasure and profit of artistic accomplishment, in cultural values and in learning the skills of solving individual and social problems.

5. ROLE OF BOOK FAIRS IN PROMOTING READING HABIT

It is now being increasingly realized that the fever of electronic media has influenced the reading habit of people in India and other Asian countries on the one hand, and the advanced technique of communication has outclassed the importance of publication world, on the other. Owing to continuous transmission of programmes through satellite channels, people find it very difficult to get time for reading or writing. In this context, the Eleventh World Book Fair held at Pragati

Maidan, New Delhi from 5th to 13th February, 1994 by the National Book Trust, assumes enormous significance.

Ever since the declaration of 1972 as an International Year of books by UNESCO, book fairs have emerged as effective means of promoting books and the habit of reading. The National Book Trust, India, organizes five to six book fairs every year in different cities. They attract a large number of visitors, and, besides generating sale of books, help in creating an environment for reading. The World Book Fair was an expression of commitment to promote books and the habit of reading, with the objective of establishing a book-reading, educated and civilized society.

The 11th World Book Fair took off with a bang on 5 Feb., '94 at the Pragati Maidan, New Delhi, with the inauguration ceremony at 11 a.m. by Shri Arjun Singh, Minister for Human Resource Development. Prof. Dennis Brutus, eminent South African poet and Mr. Henri Lopea, writer and statesman from the erstwhile Popular Republic of Congo, were the guests of honour.

Spread across nearly two square kilometres with a covered space of 28,000 square metres accommodating over a million titles on display by 964 participating publishers from the world over, and Africa as the central theme, it was a microcosm of the publishing world. Billed as the Show of the Season because there was something in it for everyone, it was the biggest book show ever put up in India and, in terms of space covered, it is being termed the biggest in Asia and the second largest (after Frankfurt) of the 37 book fairs organised in various parts of the world.

The Book Fair should project Indian publishing to promote the sale of books and translation rights. In addition, the New Delhi World Book Fair should promote publishing in Asia and Africa within the region and outside. It was in this context that it was decided to focus on Africa in the 11th New Delhi World Book Fair by arranging a special display of books and holding two seminars — "Africa and India, publishing for a New Age" and "Black Writing Across the Continents".

Jawaharlal Nehru had once remarked, "Can we solve the problems of the world by ignoring the wisdom of the people of Asia and Africa?" With Africa becoming more accessible to the outside world, this has greater relevance today than even before. It is only appropriate that the 11th New Delhi World Book Fair should focus on writing and publishing in Africa. Both India and Africa have much in common — both have complex cultures and a range of ethnically and radically diverse people belonging to virtually all the major religions of the world. This multi-cultural heritage has bestowed on Africa and India a wealth of traditional knowledge and lore.

Besides the focus on Africa, the 11th New Delhi World Book Fair had much more to offer. In addition to the special exhibit of books from Africa which had around 2,000 select titles and 60 scholarly journals published in 13 African countries, the National Book Trust had put up displays of children's books. For the children's counter the Trust had received from the Bologna International Children's Book Fair, 2,064 select books for children brought out by 302 publishers from 33 countries. In fact, the Indian Book House stall had been attracting the largest crowds, and visitors to it had to be finally regulated. The appeal lay in the fact that there was an outstanding range of books for children and an enviable range for adults. Coupled with this was the presence of Shobha De, signing her books to the delight of buyers.

A novel feature of the Fair was the splendid display of select academic and literary journals. Almost 1,600 journals relating to various fields and in different languages were on display in the first ever display of this kind. More than half of these were, however, in English and related mostly to pure and applied sciences. An annotated catalogue of the journals had also been brought out.

On top of that, organisation of seminars, workshops, presentations and thirty such other activities on subjects of concern to the book industry was an integral part of the World Book Fair. On 6 February, 1994, the National Book Trust, through its National Centre for Children's Literature held a half-day workshop on 'Low-Priced Books for Children'. The workshop was intended for those involved in bringing out reading material for children. The problems of publishing inexpensive books for children and possible solutions were discussed at the workshop by well-known publishers of children's books from the Indian languages and English. On 10, 11 and 12 February, 1994, the Trust organised workshops on Electronic Communication in the Book Trade and Book Clubs, in collaboration with the British Council Division of the British High Commission, and Indian Book Trade and the United States Market.

The National Book Trust, India and the Bharat Gyan Vigyan Samiti organised a symposium on the 'Post-Literacy Reading Material for neo-literates' on 8 February, 1994. The objective was to draw attention of publishers to the need for bringing out a large number of imaginative, entertaining and informative books for 50 to 55 million neo-literates of varied age groups and from different socio-economic backgrounds, which include 60 to 75 per cent women. It was hoped that this symposium would be the first step towards formulation of a comprehensive and co-ordinated programme to meet one of the most important publishing challenges of the time.

Thus, the 11th New Delhi World Book Fair had something for everyone. For the book industry, it was an occasion to revive old contacts, get into new partnerships, and to interact on issues vital for its development and growth. For institutional visitors and librarians it was an occasion to study new trends in publishing and buy the latest books on subjects of their interest. It was also an occasion to introduce children to reading, a gift that helps in the formation of a balanced personality.

To an individual, however, the New Delhi World Book Fair offered an excellent opportunity to purchase books on all possible subjects, in different languages. It was a treat to walk through rows and rows of stalls in different halls of Pragati Maidan, and to browse through and buy books. Though the book fair was held for nine days, it was so large that very few people were able to visit each and every stand and stall. Most of the visitors had to be content with looking at books at some select stands. However, there were some who came to the Fair every day, as it opened, and were seen leaving in the evening carrying large packets of books with them. Indeed, a rare scene nowadays.

6. THE ART OF BOOK REVIEWING

Book-reviewing is a popular intellectual exercise today. It has become a specialised but regular academic activity the world over. Also, book reviews can, and frequently do, make good reading. Well written reviews are a Joy. It is not, therefore, surprising to find certain popular weekly magazines like *New Statesman* and the *Spectator*, in the West, and *University News* in India devoting considerable space to book-reviews. Some organs such as the *London Review of Books* are totally dedicated to book-reviews. Newspapers, particularly the Sunday editions, have at least one section where well-known people review books. Besides, well-established and widely read newspapers like *The Hindu*, and *The Times of India* devote one full page to book-reviews. Book-reviews also form a part of "The Literary Review" of *The Hindu*. Academic Journals, too, both in India and abroad, devote sufficient space to book-reviews, and their reputation depends to a considerable degree on the quality of the book-reviews.

But, unlike the feature printed articles, book-reviews have usually not undergone the rigorous and often hypercritical process of peer review. Because of the unwritten law of 'publish or perish' every journal in every discipline receives many more books than it could possibly get reviewed. That is why, we have all kinds of book-reviews which are often not reliable and valid. What is worse, there are cases of stagemanaging the book reviews, by getting them done through some kind of understanding, with a view to getting an academic boost.

Some publishers and self-publicists take resort to manipulation of reviews of the books published by them. They are skilled at choosing phrases or words out of context for the dust cover or an advertisement. For instance, 'Despite the possibilities for a sensitive treatment of a profound issue, the author has proved to be completely lacking in insight and perspicacity' may become 'a sensitive treatment of a profound issue' and 'insightful and perspicacious'. John Betjeman who knew the trick warns : 'Friendly attacks should begin with faint praise, but be careful not to use adjectives or phrases of which the publisher can make use in advertisements.'

Small wonder, therefore, if some universities in the West refuse to consider books, monographs and book chapters, as admissible evidence for applications for promotion. The reason is that books have not been reviewed before publication, and post-publication reviews are not always reliable. Some publishing houses do, in fact, undertake some form of peer review, but the suspicion is that the final decisions to publish are based on commercial rather than academic grounds.

No doubt, some editors of journals and newspapers make a sincere effort to systematise review comments so that they are more reliable and valid. Some still rely on a sort of impressionistic free-response format, but more and more editors require that reviewers rate a book on a number of dimensions such as clarity of expression, economy of exposition, methodological accuracy and adequacy and theoretical importance. In doing so, they are attempting to guide reviewers to look for certain specific aspects of the book so that their task of reconciling differences between reviewers may be done by some objective, averaging, discounting or other principle. Not all editors or journals adopt the same process, but all the editors are concerned with the reliability and validity of reviews inasmuch as they inevitably relate to the quality of the books accepted and rejected and thus to the standing of the journal in the field.

There are a number of reasons why book-reviews may prove interesting and amusing, but cannot be said to be a valid and reliable assessment of the academic merits of a book. The most important reason is that book-reviewers are named, unlike peer reviewers for articles who remain anonymous. Being named, various response sets or artifacts occur that affect the way the book is reviewed irrespective of its content.

Successful and useful book-reviewing is dependent on several factors in order to ensure validity and reliability. First and foremost, one should consider who reviews books. Many have suggested that most critics and reviewers are themselves failed authors. Vladimir Nabokov wrote : sterile instructors successfully endeavour to produce by reviewing the books of more fertile colleagues. Leigh Hunt also noted : ''The critic is often an unsuccessful author, almost always an inferior one.'' Samuel Taylor Coleridge was much more blunt when he said : ''Reviewers are usually people who would have been poets, historians and biographers if they could; they tried their talents at one or at the other and have failed; therefore, they turn critics.'' Indeed, Pope's famous essay on criticism is a superb treatise on the dangers of being a reviewer. Hence, the need to choose a right and competent reviewer.

Secondly, there is the issue of the consequences of giving a positive *versus* a negative review. Just as there is general agreement about the sort of people who choose to become critics or reviewers, so there is some measure of agreement about the desirability of a negative or damning review. W.H. Auden pointed out : ''One cannot attack a bad book without showing off.'' Lambert Jeffries put it more subtly : ''There is a type of critic whose attitude suggests that the book he is reviewing was written by his kind permission, and that the author has grossly abused the privilege.''

Therefore, one need not be surprised to learn that negative evaluators are often seen as intelligent and insightful experts while positive evaluators are seen as naive, unintelligent novices. Therefore, the more one believes in this principle, the more tempted one is to offer a negative, rather than a positive review, irrespective of one's actual reactions to the book. But, both the explanations are to be rejected in favour of the simple idea that it is intellectually insecure individuals who show and admire negative criticisms. Thus, in the words of Stephen

Potter : "The critic is invariably a tremendous specialist in a subject under review, and must at all costs be more so than the author or the book discussed."

Thirdly, what matters much is not only who to choose to review the book, their expertise, availability and ability to write, but what instructions to give them? It is not unusual to receive a book through the post from the reviews editor requesting a review of not more than certain number of words and by a specified date. Thus, one may comment on the cover, the price, the type-face or any aspect of the book some of which are beyond the control of the author. To what extent should one seek out typographical errors or diagram mislabelling which, one may infer, is indicative of general sloppiness, not only of proof reading but also of the writing or thinking? Some reviewers simply discuss the merits or otherwise of the central theory of plot, while some reviewers do little more than expand on the contents page. Presumably, the reviewer is at liberty to choose any criterion that he or she wishes. Rarely, if ever, are reviewers guided or instructed as to which features of the book — comprehensiveness, originality, clarity and lay-out, — should be considered.

From this it is clear that book-reviewing is essentially an art, as much a significant art as book writing. To maintain the requisite standards, book reviews must undergo some editorial processing such as improving the language, ironing out an ambiguity or more likely being passed under the eagle eye of a libel lawyer. What is more, book-reivews must be checked for reliability. Any author may compare and contrast the reviews of his or her book and find great diversity in the length, style, criteria selected for criticism and the conclusion or verdict reached.

To make book-reviews more comprehensive, fair and comparable and less idiosyncratic and less open to bias, two basic steps must be undertaken. The first is to use more than one reviewer, who may remain anonymous, but who are known for their expertise and fair-mindedness. The second is that the potential reviewers are given specific criteria — literary expertise, critical acumen, dispassionate outlook, competence, kindness, fairness, likability and open-mindedness — upon which to judge the book. Only then the published reviews will be useful in actually evaluating a book.

VII

NON-FORMAL EDUCATION FOR EGALITARIAN SOCIETY

1. NON-FORMAL EDUCATION FOR BETTER LIVING

The major weakness of the formal system of education is that it divorces work from development, and has no relationship with productivity and aspirations of the people. This system of education has grown into a huge monolithic structure with tremendous emphasis on rigidity and conformity. Beside, the benefits from such a system of education reach only a minority of the population.

Furthermore, the formal system of education can never bring all the different age groups to school, or provide life-long education. That is why our society has developed between the well-to-do modernized elite and the poor, traditional masses. If we are to create an egalitarian society, the masses must be educated and organised so that they have their share of power to improve their standard of living.

Against this background non-formal education assumes great importance for the illiterate millions. The non-formal education programmes impart skills in reading, writing and arithmetic only to make use of them in their daily life, and to enable them to continue their education either on their own or through other available avenues of Adult Education. These programmes help the adults to interest themselves in vital national problems and to participate effectively in the social and civic activities of their community.

The non-formal education programmes are essentially work-based and, therefore, aim at creating positive attitudes and creative interests and imparting skills and information which will help the adults to do effectively whatever work they are engaged in — on the farm, in industry or office. In other words, all non-formal education programmes are integrally related to some form or the other of socially productive work thereby actively involving the people in social and national development.

On the economic front, non-formal education can help increase in productivity both in agriculture and industry. Literate workers can quickly pick up the latest methods of increasing production, and make better use of the good services. They can, thus, improve both the quality and quantity of outputs and prove themselves an asset to the management, and to the nation at large.

Socially, non-formal education programmes are in no way less fruitful. Ours is a democratic country requiring enlightened citizens who are conscious of their rights and responsibilities and who understand the values of franchise and exercise it judiciously. Non-formal education would go a long way in making the illiterate masses become aware of their rights and responsibilities as well as of the value of the vote they cast. On top of that, Adult Education can fortify the people from the age-old oppression and suppression, social injustice and all forms of exploitation, thereby enabling them to gain self-confidence and self-respect.

Through non-formal education, the concepts of healthy living can be more effectively instilled into the people. In Adult Education classes they learn the importance of cleanliness, the need for a balanced diet and the causes and cures of diseases. They can be trained in the First Aid too. Especially the women-folk who are more directly concerned with the management and planning of families will be greatly benefited by Adult Education programmes.

Non-formal Education can also be effective not only in making the people become conscious of the social evils like alcoholism, gambling, sex deviations, dowry and untouchability, but also in eradicating these evils from society through social action. Besides, the conflict of interests between the younger and older generations could be reduced by comprehensive programmes of Adult Education.

Thus, non-formal education certainly provides for better living for the millions of illiterate masses economically, socially and morally. In other words, through non-formal education an average Indian who is an illiterate for sheer lack of access to formal education could still hope for a better living, and could still be considered a man of civilization and culture.

2. LINKING EDUCATIONAL PROGRAMMES WITH THE NEEDS OF SOCIETY

The present educational system is responsible for increasing the deplorable gulf between the educated and the uneducated classes, between the intelligentsia and the masses. The intelligentsia should try to become a real service group, striving to uplift the masses and not become a parasitical group, living for itself and perpetuating its own privileged position.

Our traditional "elite" as a whole — with some noble exception — had no close ties with the masses and the new "elite" created by modern education also remained largely aloof from the people, except during the struggle for freedom under Mahatama Gandhi, when he was able to inspire a large number of educated and well-to-do persons to identify themselves with the interests of the masses and the country as a whole. But, when the struggle for freedom came to an end with the attainment of independence, the intelligentsia again tended to move away from the people.

It is, therefore, imperative that a close link is forged between the educational programme and the needs of the society. The universities and training institutions should identify themselves with the economic and social environment and develop a sense of commitment to the task of meeting the needs of the society.

The universities and colleges can involve teachers and students in a variety of social service and developmental activities side by side with the normal academic programme. Eradication of illiteracy is one of them. Illiteracy is a drag on social and economic development. If the sutdent youth both in colleges and high schools were to concentrate their efforts on eradication of illiteracy, at least, in its first phase, a big national task would have been undertaken and a great service rendered to the country. There are numerous other programmes — agricultural development, afforestation, soil conservation, slum clearance, voluntary health services, promotion of family planning programmes, child welfare, prevention of wastage of foodgrains, eradication of social evils, removal of untouchability, drought and disaster relief measures, rehabilitation of the physically handicapped, welfare of the socially handicapped, emergency relief programmes, and recreational activities which could be adopted by the student youth as part of their educational programme.

As the students draw up their different items of their Community and Social Service Programme, certain basic requirements shall have to be met. First, the programme should be worthwhile and workable. The worthwhileness is to be determined by : (a) the degree of its acceptability to the student volunteers and the community with whom they choose to work; (b) the extent of the identification of the programme with the NSS goal, or its near proximity to the latter. The practicability of the programme will depend on the availability of — (i) adequate financial resources, (ii) manpower, and (iii) expertise. These factors must be taken into account before a diversified programme is chalked out.

Participation in the Community and Social Service Programme could be made either compulsory for all students or optional for those who have a flair for social work.

If Community and Social Service Programme is to be compulsory and part of the educational programme of the students, 200 out of the total marks may be allotted to social service work. A limited number of students should be assigned to each teacher who will maintain a cumulative record of the performance of the student throughout the year and award marks accordingly. A specific number of marks may be allocated to participation in the Adult Education Programme. Each student may be asked to make at least 10 adult illiterates, literate within a year. After examining the proficiency achieved by the adults, marks may be awarded to the student accordingly.

If Community and Social Service Programme is to be made optional, it may be offered in lieu of one subject. At the undergraduate level every student has to study three different subjects under part II. Those who opt for programme could be exempted from studying one subject and the same procedure as suggested above may be followed in assessing the work done by the students.

The only alternative to the two methods suggested above is to involve the student in community service work at least for two months every year during winter and summer vacations as a pre-requisite for getting the degree he or she is studying for. For this purpose, a comprehensive, workable programme could be designed keeping in mind the immediate needs of the society around. This would enable the student at least to come in close contact with the realities of rural life.

3. OPEN UNIVERSITIES FOR UNIVERSALIZING HIGHER EDUCATION

It is imperative to realize that for a country like India it is next to impossibility to fully satisfy the ever-increasing educational demands of people through the formal system of education by way of starting more and more colleges and universities. For, the number of educational institutions can never be in proportion to the actual requirements of people with the explosion of population. Hence, the dire need for an informal and non-formal system of education which is amply met by the system of Open University.

The advent of Open University is, perhaps, the most revolutionary measure the world of education ever witnessed. Breaking fresh ground, it modified and revolutionized the concept of education and made it fit for the felt needs and rosy aspirations of the post-war generation. It is easily a breakthrough in educational technology. The very nature of this novel approach to education recommends itself to a developing country like India.

The first Open University was set up in 1969 at the town of Milton Keynes situated about 120 miles north of London. It was started with a complex of undergraduate courses preparing students of the Arts, Sciences, Technology and Social Sciences for a degree. The courses were extended later to the post-graduate level and it now offers subjects for research leading to Ph.D. The degrees of the Open University are recognized as equivalent in quality and status to those of conventional British Universities.

An Open University is one which is thrown open to one and all, irrespective of their previous qualifications, to seek knowledge and improve themselves. It is a kind of Correspondence University using a multi-media approach to its students who are conceived of as ordinary working people in farms, trades and professions all over the country, willing to work hard in their spare time in order to improve their knowledge and obtain a university degree. The only condition it prescribes is the minimum of age to a particular degree. Once this is fulfilled, one can appear for any degree with no prior formal academic qualifications. It does not matter if one has not even attended any school or college. 'Readiness is all' that is required.

The Open University is unique in the way in which it permits each individual student to select his own combination of courses, even switching, if he wishes, from Arts to Science and back, until he has built up the requisite number of credits or grades for either a pass or a distinction. Each individual course, leading to a credit or grade, is a 'package' consisting of weekly radio and fortnightly television programmes, correspondence materials, one or two contact classes, and in the case of Science students, a complex kit of apparatus, chemicals or whatever is appropriate for the home study of each particular subject.

The Open University sticks to its schedules with a ruthless promptitude. Every week the broadcast programmes have to be followed. Each is repeated a day or two after the original transmission. The correspondence materials divided into units — each unit consisting of at least 30 pages of rightly packed discussion and commentary punctuated by questions and specimen answers for periodic self-evaluation — are plopped through mail with uncanny regularity.

This is followed by the essays submitted by students to their tutors concerned. Each essay submitted will be returned, duly monitored and marked, within 10 days. The student's essay grades form a substantial part of his overall assessment. Each student has not only a tutor but also a counsellor, a second person to whom he or she could readily refer for help, especially of a non-academic kind and whose duty it is to mediate between tutor and student, should the need ever arise.

As regards other organisational aspects of the Open University's work, reference has to be made to the multiple-choice assignments which students on many courses have to complete in addition to their tutor-marked work. There is provision for monitoring each tutor's range of grades or marks to ensure that they are not more lenient or more severe than those of other tutors on the same course. A system of feed-back from tutors and students is maintained so that each set of materials and each course is constantly evaluated and revised. There is also provision for new 'post-experience' courses for teachers, social workers, and other professionals. The Open University strongly encourages the practice of 'self-help' groups organised by the students themselves.

Thus, with its vast scope and variegated functions, the Open University is what is most called for in our country at present. With its novel approach of imparting education meaningfully to a maximum number of people in a minimum amount of time through a system which is democratic to the core, the Open University goes a long way in universalizing higher education in India.

VIII

EXTENSION EDUCATION FOR COMMUNITY DEVELOPMENT

1. WORKING WITH, NOT FOR, THE PEOPLE : EXTENSION EDUCATION

When Ruskin said long back — ''education does not mean teaching people to know what they do not know; it means teaching them to behave as they do not behave'' — he at once provided the key and set the tone for Extention Education. Extension Education is an out-of-school system of education in which adults and young people learn by doing, not simply by reading and listening. In short, it is an education designed to meet the actual needs of the people so as to bring about desired changes in their knowledge, attitudes and skills with a view to helping them live better. Thus, they learn to grow better crops, keep better homes and to make better use of their resources thereby benefiting by all the knowledge that modern science and technology can provide.

It is very essential to understand the scope of Extension Education. Extension is an organisation set up to teach people and motivate them to action, but not to dictate what the people should do, and not merely to render supplies and services. In other words, it is an organisation to plan, execute and evaluate programmes *with* the people and not *for* the people, along the lines of their current interests and needs. Thus, an Extension worker becomes only a catalyst who sets up learning situations for the people and help them develop themselves.

Broadly speaking, the functions of Extension Education are to assist people to discover and analyse their problems, their felt and unfelt needs; to develop leadership among people and help them solve their problems themselves; to disseminate information based on research or practical experience in such a manner that people would grasp and accept and put it into actual practice; and to keep the research workers in the universities informed of the peoples' problems from time to time so as to facilitate their endeavour to offer solutions based on research. Thus, by changing the outlook of people and increasing their production and income, Extension Education purports to achieve the development of the community as a whole.

The first task of the Extension teacher, therefore, is to direct the attention of the people to the new or better idea. Unless the individual's attention is focused on the desired change, there is no recognition of the problem to be solved. Once the individual's attention has been focused, it becomes possible for the teacher to stimulate his interest. The stimulation of the learners' interest in the new idea or better practice has to be continued until that interest becomes a motivating force sufficiently strong to compel action. The end product of Extension Education is the achievement of the satisfaction of the worker as the result of solving a problem, meeting a need and acquiring a new skill. The satisfaction and confidence from the successful completion of a particular project will automatically lead him on to the accomplishment of further projects on his own.

The methods and techniques used for Extension teaching are (a) individual contacts, by way of farm and home visits, personal letters and result demonstrations, (b) group contacts through method demonstration meetings, leader training meetings, conferences and discussions, and (c) mass contacts through leaflets, bulletins, circular letters, exhibits, posters, charts, motion pictures, radio, television and other visual aids. Although these methods and techniques are applicable to any community, locality or village, they should necessarily be adjusted to suit the social, economic, physical and intellectual levels of the people and the requirements of the situations that confront the Extension worker.

The Extension teacher thus plans, arranges and executes situations and activities in living contact with the rural youth in such a manner as to arouse and stimulate their interest, create their conviction, prompt their action and promote their satisfaction. He works with them to help them develop themselves and achieve better personal well-being. To conclude with Kelsey and Hearne, "The philosophy of Extension work thrives best in the man or woman who holds a deep concern for the well-being of all mankind and an abiding faith in rural people and their ability to develop and reach the highest planes."

2. CASE FOR CONSUMER EDUCATION

Perhaps, the most exploited entity, in the world in general and in India in particular, is the consumer who is a helpless, sad spectator in the drama of inflation, adulteration, profiteering, price-hike and what not. He is a victim not only of many malpractices perpetrated by the unscrupulous, greedy businessman, but also of several self-deceptions. Especially in a country like India with a high degree of illiteracy of the masses, and even a higher degree of economic illiteracy among the educated classes, inequalities and exploitation of the weak by the strong are inherent in the working of the market structures. Besides, the widespread imperfections and oligopolies in retail markets, an organised sector which has developed techniques of defrauding both the government and the consumer and, above all, a rather low level of business morality and social responsibility have made the things worse.

Moreover, the consumer has become increasingly dependent upon the manufacturer, the trader and the advertiser for advice and guidance on the right choice and quality of goods. As a result, a number of problems have cropped up, problems of widespread adulteration of food supplies, highly exploitative market mechanisms of sale of essential commodities, wrong weights and measures, profiteering at all levels, black marketing and the use of advertising media for misguiding the gullible and ignorant consumers. Either the government is unable to protect the consumer, or the concern for legalities does not permit it to adopt certain techniques of control over the economy. What is more, despite the poor quality of goods, large scale adulteration and profiteering, the consumers in our country have not felt the need to organise themselves into effective forum. Every one is fed up, but nobody wants to take the initiative and do the needful.

It is in this context that Consumer Education becomes a very important function of social action. The goal of consumer education is to make the consumer a skilful and intelligent buyer by way of creating necessary awareness and building up necessary Consumer resistance in him against unscrupulous traders and trade practices, through mass media and other available methods of communication and dialogue. Thus, consumer education aims at protecting the interests of the consumer in ensuring that goods are made available to him in good quality at reasonable prices, in right time and at right place.

Consumer Education could be imparted not only through mass media and consumer councils, but also through schools, colleges and

Adult Education Centres. Courses on Consumer Education could be introduced as part of school curriculum thereby making it relevant to the felt needs of society. Traditionally schools and colleges have been thought of as places where young people prepare themselves to earn living by acquiring necessary knowledge and skills to enable them to enter a trade or profession. Now some educators rightly urge that equal emphasis should be laid on students' learning to spend money skilfully and wisely.

Students should, therefore, be educated on budgeting, money management, basic facts about nutrition and many other problems related to everyday living. He must also be taught how to cope with situations that arise in the market place, how to read labels and follow advertisements, how to get information about the quality of goods and services and thus acquire buying skills. One should not lose sight of the fact that preparing the student to become a future family purchasing agent is no mean task, but an integral part of the education process.

3. NSS : A UNIQUE EXPERIMENT IN MAKING HIGHER EDUCATION MEANINGFUL

Ever since Independence we have been talking of the need to transform our educational system, but we have consistently lacked the courage to embark on a revolutionary plan of action. The principal malady has been the built-in puritanical academicism in the universities. Despite the deep concern expressed about the immediate relevance of higher education, necessary steps have not been taken either by the University Grants Commission, or by the universities to grapple with the issue of restructuring old courses, whereby linkage between the socio-economic development of the community and the educational goals of the university could be established.

The realization that the educational system should be socially meaningful and relevant brought into being the present National Service Scheme (NSS) which has opened up new vistas for the institutions of higher learning to become instruments of social transformation and development. Almost every university in the country has the N.S.S. unit and the Government is spending considerbale amount of money in running these units. Each N.S.S. student volunteer is expected to put in during his leisure hours of his career 120 hours of social work per year besides participating in the Dasara, Pongal and Summer camps, by laying roads, planting trees, digging canals and cleaning slums and villages. Furthermore, the NSS volunteers are expected to play a meaningful role "with an abiding concern for the well-being of the underprivileged, weak and poor" by recapturing the spirit of idealism which inspired our people during the freedom struggle. This is precisely what the Father of the Nation wanted.

The catalytic role that the NSS volunteers have to play in community welfare could be three-fold : (1) diffusion of knowledge among the masses; (2) involvement in the productive processes of the community; and (3) rendering socially useful service to the local community and the nation at large.

Diffusion of Knowledge

The NSS volunteers can disseminate knowledge, which they have acquired in the university, among the masses, so that the latter may lead a better life. The community provides facilities to them and in return the students should help the people in their economic and social uplift. This can be done in several ways by (a) running adult literacy classes; (b) teaching the needy children in spare times; (c) arranging popular talks on developments in science, government policies, international relations, sanitation, hygiene and such other subjects of common interest with a view to enabling the masses to live as responsible citizens; (d) giving demonstrations of better methods and techniques of cultivation, food preservation, kitchen-rearing, health, sanitation and other household jobs; and (e) providing information about and giving demonstration of improved methods and techniques of earning livelihood. Thus, the students can put their knowledge of the subject earned in universities and colleges to a social use thereby enabling the community to perform their vocational activities in a more scientific manner.

Involvement in Productive Processes

The NSS student volunteers could be involved in the productive processes of the nation in the following ways : (a) assisting the community in the construction of places of community service such as a school building, a dispensary or a link road; (b) helping farmers to fight against pests; (c) getting protected water supply to the rural masses; (d) making the local industries develop welfare centres for the workers; (e) constructing centres of recreation for the village community; (f) preparation of play fields for the parental institution; (g) assisting the community to improve sanitary conditions; (h) plantation of trees and their care; and (i) assisting neighbouring schools in preparing school equipment, furniture and teaching apparatus.

Rendering Welfare Service to Community

Besides participation in the productive processes, the NSS volunteers need involve themselves in rendering useful service to the community outside. Through involvement in the services of the community, a student gains psychological satisfaction. It is psychologically very much satisfying to have performed a noble act. Doing service to the community helps one to identify one's interests with those of the community served. Activities pertaining to community service can be as follows : (a) doing some of the jobs, which are attended to at present by lower staff members, such as cleaning one's own room in the hostel, self-serving in the canteen and decorating the college campus; (b) helping the community in fighting against drought, famine and epidemics; (c) running community services in a co-operative manner such as running a co-operative consumer society, issuing books from the students' library and running a co-operative mess; (d) assisting government in maintaining peace and order during emergency; (e) maintaining order during fairs and holding exhibitions; (f) preparing the people to defend the country against internal and external threats; (g) helping Government in fighting against social evils such as drinking, gambling, black-marketing, bribery, dowry and corruption; and (h) participating in community development programmes.

If the goal of N.S.S. is to create a new social consciousness and to re-dedicate student energies and talents to problems in national development thereby making education meaningful, then an optional, periodical NSS programme is by itself not an answer. The objective of the NSS could be realized fully only by making the NSS an integral part of the curriculum. This means that the syllabi of the various courses of study are to be so restructured that the entire educational effort becomes a vehicle for identifying the problems of social development and for fostering the requisite skills and orientations that can be brought to bear on their solution.

Although educators have accepted in principle the need for reorientation of education, the Boards of Studies and the other academic bodies try to postpone action on the ground of the lack of resources, or of sheer impracticability of the proposal, without even examining the issue in all seriousness that it really deserves. Mental barriers rather than the constraint of financial sources seem to pose a great problem.

It is high time the NSS was integrated into the subject syllabi itself by way of blending classroom teaching with practical work in the community setting on an inter-disciplinary basis. Each discipline should plan its curriculum with a view to identifying, from its special point of view, the social problems that clamour for solution, cultivate the requisite skills to attack these problems, and from these two bases enhance the frontiers of human knowledge.

Thus, the integration of NSS with the curriculum will arouse the social conscience of students, imbue them with a sense of social commitment and enable them to put the education they receive to a social use. The process not only seeks to make education pruposeful and meaningful but senitizes the members of the university community, who are a privileged group, to contribute their mite to the good of the society. Thus, proper implementation of NSS in colleges and universities by making it an integral part of the curriculum would go a long way in making education really meaningful and relevant to the felt needs of the community, a dire need of the hour, indeed!

4. N.S.S. AS AN AGENT OF HUMAN RESOURCE DEVELOPMENT

The establishment of the National Service Scheme, involving thousands of students as well as the non-student youth of diverse cultural backgounds and academic orientations, with its remarkable growth within the short span of twenty years, is indicative of a constructive urge motivating the student of today to find channels of self-involvement in the affairs of his society and to seek opportunities of fuller deveopment of his personality.

The significance of the NSS as an agent of human resource development naturally springs from the role of higher education in national reconstruction as well as from the psychological need of having a sense of participation in nation-building tasks. Today, the NSS constitutes the only vehicle for the student community to channelize their energies for social action to reconstruct both education and environment. It is the most meaningful development that has come upon the Indian university campuses and has within it catalytic potentialities bringing to function the long-felt urgent reforms in education and ridding it of its colonial shackles.

The NSS volunteers have been engaged in a great variety of nation-building activities. However, there is so much to be done anywhere and any time in our country that the area of national service becomes almost limitless. No activity, however small, with a bearing on the improvement of the conditions of existence of the exploited masses can be taken to be out of place.

The concept of national service is increasingly receiving attention in the universities all over the world. It is assuming proportions of a real mass movement in the developing countries, particularly those which have emancipated themselves from imperialist bondage.

The need for work orientation in the course of studies and temperamental craving to be of help to others have invariably placed emphasis on the individual and have tended to ignore the social reality. It is, therefore, appropriate that the focus should have shifted to the total human environment of which education is an integral part. It is this environment that is now sought to be transformed by using education as one of the chief instruments.

Thus, the National Service Scheme, which is essentially an educational programme, is eminently suited to be a significant agent of human resource development. Let us hope and believe that the NSS would make bigger strides in human resource development and become an integral part of the university curriculum so that each department of study would plan its curriculum with a view to identifying social problems and cultivating the requisite skills to solve the problems and, from these two bases, enhance the frontiers of human knowledge.

5. EDUCATION FOR NATIONAL INTEGRATION

India today sits on a smouldering volcano in which the fratricidal conflicts between difficult religions, castes, communities and linguistic groups are reaching a point of explosion. The call of the hour is to break all barriers dividing our people, and weave a true unity of hearts in the cause of a new India.

India is a poly-cultural and multi-social Nation. We have a heritage of cultural and social developments that would outdo any other country. The trailing socio-cultural tradition of India takes us back to the Mohenjo-Daro-Harappa days and leaves us with a recorded socio-cultural history of thirty centuries. It is, therefore, no wonder that we have a rich heritage of such socio-cultural diversity in India. National integration alone can tap in the right way this resource of socio-cultural diversity and channel it for national development.

India as a country is, therefore, compelled to emphasise national integration because the country's very survival depends on and is conditioned by the unity among the large number of constituent States and among the variety of factors and forces that keep the country divided. National integration as a value assumes a new dimension against the background of the diversity and multiplicity that are characteristics of our National life. India is primarily a multilingual nation. The fourteen constitutionally endorsed languages and about two hundred regional, local non-constitutional languages constitute a spectrum that has influenced greatly the formation and progress of our Nation. The States are constituted primarily on the basis of our languages. The same multilingual diversity is at the root of most of our problems even after nearly five decades of independence. National integration is the only principle that can enforce unity amidst this diversity.

II

Forces of Disintegration

Let us analyse the forces which tend to disintegrate the none-too-strong fabric of our national faith and fervour and then suggest a few integrative measures necessary for connecting our people purposefully regardless of their religion, region, language, caste and political affiliation.

Communalism, revivalism, regionalism, linguism, secessionism and casteism are the divisive forces that are eating into the vitals of National integration. To these have recently been linked two other factors — uneven economic growth and the ever-widening gulf between the rich and the poor.

Communalism which is spreading like wild fire at present is the most dangerous parochial divisive force. Pandit Nehru called it a 'bigoted approach'. Communalism is a direct child of secular politics deprived of normative content. Religious sentiments of people are roused to serve politic end. Many lives of innocent people are being sacrificed.

Regionalism is another divisive force to be combated effectively. Various states in India continue fighting over trivial issues like the distribution of river water, administration of a small chunk of territory, the sharing of resources and key industries, unmindful of the damage their unseemly conflicts cause to the movement of national integration.

'Linguistic nationalism', to use Toynbee's phrase, threatens to become the seed-bed of disintegration. It is now being used as a smokescreen behind which prejudices and grudges are fostered. Small-minded people surface to power on the tide of linguistic fanaticism.

Caste, which in the pre-Independence days could be dismissed as a harmless social institution, based not only on the division of labour, but also on "the division of labourers", as Dr. Ambedkar rightly put it, has come to exert an insidious impact. The country is divided not only vertically between the Hindus and the Muslims, but also horizontally into numerous ethnic and pressure groups and separate class identities. Even the highly educated are unable to rise above caste considerations and judge people and things objectively.

The imbalanced economic growth creates suspicions and hostility between different regions and different sections of society in the country. The backwardness of a particular region is bound to act as a drag on the progress of comparatively affluent regions. In a democratic social order conspicuous affluence and grinding poverty cannot co-exist.

III

Integrative Measures

In spite of our repeated declarations and endeavours to promote national integration, much remains to be done. New divisive forces which seem to have emerged are becoming stronger day by day, and they must be overcome. In this context, measures for National integration become even more necessary for our National survival.

India as a nation has been endowed with an infinite capacity not only to absorb alien shock but also to surge ahead as a living organism. Our culture has been potent enogh to assimilate many foreign influences, while retaining its pristine glory. The so-called provincial sub-cultures are only the variants of one basic Indian culture. We have got to impose a homogenising and universalising conception of India on our pluralist, multi-minority population.

Common Language

It is admitted generally that India desperately needs a common link language. We cannot afford to chase away English until we are prepared for a smooth switchover to an Indian language. We can set up more Central Universities which could teach through English, but at the same time, introduce Hindi extensively. We have much to learn from the educational experiences of such countries as Japan, Israel, Sweden and Yugoslavia. The best way in the present circumstances is to implement speedily the three-language formula both in letter and in spirit.

Above all, educational institutions have a special role to play in developing a sense of National unity and National cohesion. The massive infrastructure of the educational institutions — students and teachers — have to be utilised for promoting National integration. Students are full of energy and idealism. Education should instil in the minds and hearts of our students a spirit of patriotism, a sense of self-respect, self-confidence, courage and fearlessness. It must create in them a spirit of service and the will to uplift the poor and the downtrodden. Teachers can play a vital role in cultivating and promoting the spirit of National integration.

Today numerous vistas are open for the realisation and development of the spirit of National integration. The foremost among these are the National Service Scheme (NSS), the National Cadet Corps (NCC), Scout Organisations and numerous other service organisations across the country which create in individuals a deep sense of unity and integrity amidst all the diverse elements that divide the Nation.

A firm commitment to the principle of primary loyalty to the Motherland, respect for common ancestry and future destiny as explicitly enshrined in our Constitution are our inspiring guidelines which would render petty considerations and separatist tendencies irrelevant and insignificant. In the same way, self-alienated communities and sub-cultures should get reconciled with the ethos and characterisation of the National society so that our norms and forms of action and appreciation remain identical and uniform in operation and impact.

National integration is a spirit and an awareness that needs to be developed in every citizen of the country for whom the Nation is just one and undivided. The spirit delineated as a value will enable every Indian to supersede the forces of regionalism, parochialism and communalism. National integration has to be a mass movement where people of all faiths, religions, castes and creeds will work unitedly in safeguarding the unity, integrity and sovereignty of India.

6. ROLE OF INTER-UNIVERSITY YOUTH FESTIVALS IN NATIONAL INTEGRATION

Tolstoy wrote in *Anna Karenina* that happy families resembled one another, whereas each unhappy family was unhappy in its own way. We might similarly be inclined to say that, whereas the state of integration, stability and well-being would be the same in all societies, discontent, disintegration, and rebellion would bestow a distinctive individuality on each of them, and the turbulence and disintegration of each would be different from that of others. Never before did discontent, turbulence and disintegration assume such alarming proportions in India society as at present.

India as a country is, therefore, compelled to emphasise national integration because the country's very survival depends on and is conditioned by the unity among the large number of constituent States and among the variety of factors and forces that keep the country divided. National integration as a value assumes a new dimension against the background of the diversity and multiplicity that are characteristics of our national life. India is primarily a multilingual nation. The fourteen constitutionally endorsed languages and about two hundred regional, local, non-constitutional languages constitute a spectrum that has influenced greatly the formation and progress of our nation. The States are constituted primarily on the basis of our languages. The same multilingual diversity is at the root of most of our problems even after five decades of Independence. National integration is the only principle that can enforce unity amidst this diversity.

Besides, India is poly-cultural and multi-social nation. We have a heritage of cultural and social developments that would outdo any other country. The trailing socio-cultural tradition of India takes us back to the Mohenjo-Daro-Harappa days and leaves us with a recorded socio-cultureal history of thirty centuries. It is, therefore, no wonder that we have a heritage of such socio-cultural diversity in India as to function as a principle of a great national disharmony. National integration alone can tap in the right way this resource of socio-cultural diversity and channel it for national development.

Inter-University Youth Festivals have been playing a pivotal role in furthering the noble cause of National integration, ever since their resurrection in 1985 by the Association of Indian Universities (AIU) after a gap of more than two decades. Sponsored by the Department of Youth Affairs and Sports, Government of India, the Youth Festivals have made a significant impact upon the youth by promoting in them an awareness of our historical and cultural heritage and imbuing them with a feeling of pride and national identity. This helps project their talents in varied cultural activities as the youth are congregated under one umbrella from different parts of the country, thereby deriving inspiration to fight against regionalism, communalism, casteism, linguistic chauvinism and other fissiparous tendencies.

The Youth Festivals used to be held earlier at the Talkatora Gardens, Delhi, and were discontinued in the mid-sixties owing to some circumstances beyond control. Many of the participants of those festivals are the well-known artists of music and dance of today's world. After a gap of two decades, the AIU resurrected this activity in 1985, the International Year of Youth (IYY). Till now the Association has organized twentythree Inter-University Zonal and National Festivals in various parts of this vast land.

There cannot be a better meeting place for National integration than the Youth Festivals where the youth from different parts of the country are gathered to show their talent and share their joy, love and peace. True to our rich tradition of viewing the whole country as one family, such Youth Meets enable our talented young men and women to make contacts and close links with one another, thereby promoting National integration, cultural unity and democratic values. Keeping this in mind and as a part of its continued efforts in promoting youth cultural activities, AIU organizes a series of four Inter-University Zonal Youth Festivals and one National Youth Festival every year in different universities spread over different parts of the country.

As per a nearly drawn programme, universities falling in their particular zones are extended invitation by the host universities concerned to participate with a maximum of 30 participants in the Inter-University Zonal Festivals. Subsequently the selected participants from the Zonal Youth Festivals are invited to participate in the Inter-University National Youth Festival (IUNYFEST). The Youth Festival consists of five major cultural evens — Music, Dance, Theatre, Literary Activity and Fine Arts — which are further divided into eighteen sub-events. An important requirement of the cultural events of One Act Plays, Skits, Mime, Group Song and Fine Arts is to project fundamental values of Indian culture by displaying values oriented towards the unity and integration of our country, namely, truth, devotion and loyalty. The objective of projection of such values is to help eliminate obscurantism, religious fanaticism, violence, superstition and fatalism which have become major obstacles to National development and human progress.

The following aims and objectives have been envisaged by AIU's Cultural Division in organization of the Inter-University Youth Festivals:

1. To promote and encourage art and culture amongst the youth.
2. To create awareness and a sense of pride amongst the youth to recognise and appreciate our rich cultural heritage, thereby promoting unity, amity and integration.
3. To provide a forum to the young artists to display their artistic excellence and exuberance.

4. To provide an opportunity to the youth to meet on a common platform to exhibit in friendly atmosphere excellence in music, dance, theatre, literary activities and fine arts.
5. To bring about cultural integration through the process of cultural exchange of students from diverse regions of the Indian sub-continent.
6. To provide an opportunity to the youth for healthy interaction with each other especially in the domain of art and culture and develop fellowship and friendship.
7. To enhance the capacity of university youth for aesthetic appreciation and refinement of the finer values of life.
8. To foster dynamism and creativity in the youth and enable them to contribute constructively to the achievement of social and national goals.
9. To channelise the energies and talents of youth in constructive pursuits.
10. To inculcate a spirit of adventure, cooperation and excellence by acquainting the youth with our rich cultural heritage.

The youth symbolise power, idealism and adventure. Their organized efforts can help promote nationally accepted goals and values for combating social evils which are stumbling blocks to healthy development of the nation. The Inter-University Youth Festivals are a tribute to our youth who symbolise courage, initiative, exuberance and dynamism. As Mr. S.K. Agrawala, former Secretary, AIU, rightly points out, these regularly held Youth Festivals "help instil in the youth an awareness and respect for our historical and cultural heritage and to imbue them with a sense of pride and National identity". Besides, providing an opportunity to the youth for a healthy interaction with each other and enhancing the capacity of the youth for aesthetic appreciation, "the Youth Festivals enable them to contribute constructively to the achievement of social and national goals". The Youth Festivals will provide our exuberant youth an opportunity to make them familiar with our glorious cultural heritage and channelize their energies and talents in constructive pursuits.

Inter-University Youth Festivals are the quintessence of the harmonic blend of varied Indian sub-cultures as they develop the roots of National integration, thereby inculcating an awareness in the youth of the essential similarity and fundamental values of our diverse cultures.

As Mr. Sampson David, Senior Cultural Officer, AIU, rightly observes, "In today's world of war and insecurity, these youth, cultural festivals are a silver lining in the clouded sky as the young vibrant representatives of varied backgrounds and cultures perform together, eat together, learn together and thus forge the bonds of friendship which stretches over space and time."

The organization of Inter-University Youth Festivals which have become synonymous with National integration has really been the most fascinating and challenging venture of the Association of Indian Universities. And, it must be said to the credit of A.I.U. that it has been doing its best in providing a forum to our budding artists among the student youth, coming from different backgrounds and different parts of the country, to display their artistic and histrionic talent at a common place, thereby promoting and fostering National integration in a greater measure than many other institutions in the country.

No doubt, the AIU Cultural Committee, consisting of senior Vice-Chancellors, cultural experts and senior officials from the Ministry concerned, is endeavouring to introduce innovative measures to improve the quality and stature of the Youth Festivals. What, however, remains to be done is to make the Youth Festivals more and more socially purposeful, more and more meaningful and relevant to the felt needs of the community. Hitherto, the stress seems to have been on the Indian culture and heritage. The need of the hour is to gear the various cultural events to subserve a social purpose with a view to arresting the cancerous growth of superstition and corruption at all levels. Almost every cultural item should aim at putting an end to the enormous social evils which are eating into the vitals of Indian society today. The focus should be on rousing the social conscience of the youth so as to make them develop a sense of commitment to take the country forward socially and scientifically. The ultimate goal of the Youth Festivals should be social enlightenment and not mere entertainment. The thematic content and the artistic treatment of the cultural items should be so oriented as to enable every participant in the Youth Festivals to return home with profit and delight.

IX

TOWARDS RIGHT KIND OF EDUCATION

1. BREAKING THE DICHOTMY BETWEEN TRADITIONAL AND MODERN APPROACHES TO EDUCATION

Education has been passing through a cross-fire of conflicting aims from time immemorial. The old-timers maintain that education should only perform the traditional functions of advancing scholarship, polishing personality and building character. But the modern educationists, laying emphasis on the utilitarian aspect of education, insist that education should be job-oriented, need-based and production-centred.

These apparently contradictory objectives of education are not irreconcilable. For, it is perfectly legitimate to expect the student to earn his living by learning the necessary skills and also to acquire culture which consists in the harmonious development of the human spirit whose chief ingredients are — search for truth, cultivation of beauty and practice of virtue. On completion of his academic course, the student must be able to step into professional life, fully equipped with life's know-how and job skills. At the same time, he should be in a position to sustain the human element in an increasingly impersonal society. For, the man who knows how to split the atom, but has no love in his heart becomes a monster.

What education should, therefore, aim at is producing the man who possesses both culture and mastery of knowledge in some special direction. He should possess sufficient knowledge and wisdom to realise that mere mechanics of living cannot be the sole vocation of the human spirit, and that technical knowledge alone cannot resolve the inner psychological pressures and tensions of life.

As Jiddu Krishna Murthy puts it, "the right kind of education is the awakening of intelligence and the fostering of an integrated view of life'. So, the truly educated man, who cannot be selfish and narrow-minded, is freed from the chains of degrading reality, and he develops a human outlook. He approaches life with intelligence and sympathetic understanding. He tackles controversial issues with the temper of a judge rather than that of an advocate or the notorious, expert witness. He resists the trivializing influences of society and the effects of a nervous and mindless culture which craves for sensory satisfaction. He judges things by standards which reject what is false and second-rate in life and weighs all evidence in the scales of a balance which are not tricked, biased or tilted to one side. In short, he is a successful and a socially well-adjusted citizen with character, personal rectitude, creative thinking and capacity for co-operation.

To achieve this, the instructional methods should be revamped and restructured to enable the student to develop the faculty of thinking and reasoning along with the capacity to retain the true spirit of academic disciplines. For this purpose, teaching should be suited to the inclusion of a spirit of enquiry and geared to cultural ends beyond those of vocational training. Our centres of learning should not only remain islands of purity in a sea of corruption and erosion of human values, but also generate resistance to all such evil influences. They should promote 'aggressive goodness' and 'militant co-operation'.

These are all values which flow from the daily give-and-take and the sharing of life and experience from the free and informal meetings of students and teachers by a sort of catalytic process on and off the university campus. These qualities are acquired through personal experience and practice, and through the influence of the teacher as an individual. This cannot be achieved with tapes and films, not even with programmed learning unsupplemented by the personal dimension of the teacher who gives the student the fruit of his knowledge and experience which is not found in books. In the hands of a good teacher, the text book transcends the limitations of the syllabus and shows immense possibilities.

2. BRIDGING THE GAP BETWEEN EDUCATION AND LIFE

The whims of our bureaucrats who frame our educational policies, the wooden approach of our institutional heads, the oppressive, impersonal attitude of our teachers and, above all, the staleness of content have made the present education what it is — dull, drab, insipid, meaningless and irrelevant to the context of life. Education today provides little more than a trade mark, attesting to a person's having undergone an accepted period in formal training in his special subject.

Furthermore, education today has been reduced to nothing but a systematic training in competitiveness rather than co-operation, cramming of factual data rather than experimental learning, periodical pumping in and pumping out of information rather than inculcation of a genuine spirit of inquiry and a parrot-like mouthing of opinions and conclusions arrived at by others rather than forming opinions and arriving at conclusions using all the innovative and imaginative resources that human beings have at their command right within them. As a result, education today seems to have little bearing on the physical, social and emotional lives of people. It has lost its relevance to life and has become a source of drudgery.

There are, as James T. Adams has said, obviously two educations — one to teach 'how to make a living', and the other 'how to live'. While both these aspects need equal emphasis in the imparting of education, we see that great stress has been laid on 'how to make a living' at the cost of learning 'how to live'. The training in 'how to live' has been totally neglected.

The human being starts to lose touch with himself as he receives his education first at the hands of his parents, and later from his teachers at various levels. These big people around him teach him facts and figures much more than necessary. Sometimes, they stereotype him into set patterns of behaviour, so as to conform to the accepted pattern, in the social fabric, leaving him little scope for creative experimentation and self-discovery under the burden of demands and expectations. His innate drive to explore, experiment, innovate and discover gets stifled in the process, and the end-result may be a confused human being doing what he 'ought' to be doing, simultaneously experiencing varied pull within himself from those stifled basic needs and drives.

One can hope to extricate oneself from such a stifling atmosphere by learning how to live. The phrase, 'how to live', is to be understood, first, as a process of awareness about the uniqueness of every human being. It is essential to know what one is made up of, what makes one tick, how one relates oneself to others, how one manipulates other people and gets manipulated by them in an effort to live one's life based on some early decisions one made for oneself. One can then redecide on the basis of one's newly acquired awareness on 'how to live'. So, how to live does not involve being told by the educators what to do, and what not to do. Rather, it is a process of learning to get in touch with one's innermost fibre and being alert to what happens both inside and outside, and reclaiming the unique potential that is the birthright of every individual.

With this kind of awareness as the foundation of all education, the superstructure whatever it be, will weather any storm and still remain effective. With both the teacher and the taught becoming aware of and getting in touch with their inner potential, their innate inquisitiveness, innovative abilities and zest for living and learning, the turmoil that exists today can give way to a more rewarding and more meaningful approach to and understanding of the two aspects of education — how to make a living and how to live.

3. EDUCATION FOR HUMAN RESOURCE DEVELOPMENT

Recent findings in theoretical physics and biology emphasize that there are 'limits to growth' of knowledge of the physical environment. The physical scientists assert that in several of the most sophisticated technologies we cannot go far beyond their present achievements, not because of deficiencies in know-how, but by reason of limitations inherent in natural laws. In short, we have almost come to a dead-end with regard to the tapping of material resources.

The time has now come to discover and apply the inner human resources in order to explore what is and to create what has never been. Most of our creative energy and financial resources have all along been directed to technical rather than to human innovation. We seem to be more concerned with making better things than better people. The question that we may pursue is not simply how we can produce more, faster and at less cost, but how we can learn more about human nature and talents so that technology becomes man's servant and not his master.

Modern psychology reveals that man has hitherto unsuspected and untapped resources of a versatile kind. Many potentialities of human nature have been identified by psychologists. Some of them are extra sensory perception (ESP), achievement motive and creativity. Creativity as a significant mode of intellectual potentiality has recently been identified by Prof. J.B. Guilford. Creativity is concerned with divergent ways of finding solutions to the problems as opposed to seeking one 'correct' answer through what is termed a convergent mode of thinking.

Today, we need men given not only to good judgement but also to originality and creativity. We need men who not only solve problems but find problems ahead of time. Problems exist because we have not thought of them before. So, what we need is anticipatory thinking. We do have men of creative abilities who possess distinct motivational characteristics. They have to be identified and properly encouraged. As Arnold Toynbee has rightly pointed out, "To give a fair chance to potential creativity is a matter of life and death for any society .... because the outstanding creative ability of a fairly small percentage of the population is mankind's ultimate capital asset."

Efforts to motivate, train or develop human potentialities require great ingenuity. No ready-made technique is available for realization of potentialities, especially in the case of creative potentiality. The best course under the present circumstances is to create an awareness in the individuals of their talents. Not only an individual has, within himself, vast resources, but he has resources for self-understanding. Providing opportunities for a wide variety of experiences and a climate of facilitative psychological attitudes, and involving the personnel in planning the development of the organisation will go a long way in providing 'catalytic effect' on the creative individual.

Awareness of one's potentialities can be created through a number of psychological techniques such as T-group training, Sensitivity Training, Brain Storming Technique, Bionics, Synectics and Transactional Analysis (TA). These techniques help to free creative expression from conscious and unconscious inhibitions. Furthermore, group dynamics, involving heterogeneous members, might facilitate a congenial atmosphere for the bringing out of hidden talents and latent potentialities.

To develop human resources and faculties, emphasis should also be laid on power motivation and extension motivation. Power motivation helps a person to use his influence in developing competence and power over other people. Extension motivation is reflected in the concern one has for other human beings, and for the society and group of which he is a member. Such psychological re-education to emphasize extension motivation through motivation development programmes, using feedback as the basic approach, can be very effective in the transition of our society from a grim today to a grand tomorrow.

4. TOWARDS HUMANIZING SCIENCE EDUCATION

The most frequent criticism levelled against scientists and technologists is that they normally display, with rare exceptional eases, a narrowness of view and interests, and that they are not effective as members or leaders of a team because of their inability to communicate with others or to enter sufficiently well into their thoughts and feelings. The narrow outlook and the lack of human communication on the part of the majority of modern scientists and technologists may be related largely to the very kind of education they receive.

In our science education there is excessive concentration on factual details, and the whole emphasis is on the utilitarian, the mechanical and the practical. This naturally retards the development of creative and imaginative faculties and the appreciation of the beautiful in life. Hence, the need to temper science education with humanistic disciplines.

Humanities are generally defined as human experiences refracted, reflected and represented through the verbal arts of literature, philosophy and history, the visual arts of painting, sculpture, architecture and dance, and the tonal art of music. Some would include even social sciences like economics, politics, sociology and psychology in the humanities.

With their intrinsic values, humanities will play a vital role in science and technical education in making the professionally competent men and women broad-minded men and women and large-hearted, and thus socially viable citizens. If a modern scientist or technologist is to understand the world beyond his professional interests, if he is to be made aware of the broad range of human endeavours and achievements and develop respect and appreciation for them, then he needs to be exposed, in sufficient breadth and depth to the nature and functions of various humanistic disciplines.

Man is not a simple problem that can be solved only by science. Tension, anxiety, lack of fulfilment, restlessness, doubt, disillusionment, fear of death, immortality — these are the problems that cannot be solved by scientists. Literature, art, history and philosophy, on the other hand, give man understanding, a scale of values, imagination and also wisdom.

Literature which is but the 'autobiography of humanity' enables one to discover the perennial literary themes that unite all men. Literature also helps a scientist's transcendental awareness in the midst of persuasive secularism and myopic scientism.

The science student should also be acquainted with history and philosophy so that he can live in a world of many dimensions, a world of human experience stretching across centuries. History illumines man's spiritual nature and records his secular achievements and failures. Philosophy promotes a tolerant and judicial temperament. It brings about an appreciation of the complexity of human nature and the multi-dimensional nature of human affairs.

Therefore, science education must needs be humanised by way of tempering science education with humanities like literature, history and philosophy. Then only shall we have scientists and engineers who are not intellectual cripples or social misfits, but broad-minded, large-hearted, tolerant and sympathetic citizens. Then only will the scientists and the technologists begin to see that their pursuits are but part of an integrated, larger socio-cultural complex.

5. NEED FOR VALUE-ORIENTED EDUCATION

There has been a global acceptance of the need to strengthen the content of education relating to humanistic, ethical, moral and cultural values in education, in formal systems as well as in non-formal systems. It is generally being accepted that solution to some of the most serious crises — discrimination, poverty, exploitation, and marginalisation of people — are to be found not only in eradication of ignorance about these crises through knowledge, but also in inculcation of human and moral values in the minds of students and teachers.

The University Grants Commission, through its policy frame on "Development of Higher Education in India," has advocated the need for 'value education'. Furthermore, it has been making consistent efforts to create an academic consciousness suited to value-oriented education. The recent conference of Vice-Chancellors organized by the Association of Indian Universities at Pondicherry University has also brought to focus the need for readjustments in the curriculum in order to make education a forceful tool for the cultivation of social and moral values.

Since the objective of education is the development of personality of the individual so that he or she may play a meaningful and effective role in the development of the society and the country, education has got to be value-oriented. However, value-oriented education should not be equated with moral education. It has a wider connotation and includes values of physical education, social education, mental education, aesthetic education, ethical education and spiritual education. Value-oriented education should particularly include subjects like International Understanding and Peace, Human Rights, Indian Culture and Social and Economic Justice. Value orientation does not merely imply an intellectual discussion on the theme of value as an integral part of the syllabus in various disciplines, but the practice of those values in the day-to-day life by the students and teachers.

No doubt, the New Education Policy embodies the aspirations of a national consensus to infuse values into the contents of our educational inputs. While explicitly value education is indicated in the New Education Policy, implicitly it is emphasised throughout the Policy Statement. Thus, the entire New Education Policy is, in a way, a declaration of intention to make our educational system value-based.

But, in spite of the importance attached to value education, it is likely to remain a pious paper-plan, unless we are in a position to undertake with determination effective measures to implement the policy decision at all levels. Therefore, it is imperative to develop a sound methodology for impartation and evaluation of value education.

There are three entities involved in any value education programme — the teacher, the student and the society. The contents of teaching, the example the teacher is able to provide, and the way the instruction is carried out are important aspects of good teaching. Equally important are the qualities of receptivity, motivation and the capacity to comprehend on the part of the student. The efficient performance of the roles of the teacher and student depend on the family and the overall social situation in which the teaching-learning situation takes place. Thus, the essential prerequisites of value education are exemplary teachers, motivated students and a favourable socio-cultural milieu.

The quality of the teacher and the standards of our teaching are, indeed, at a very low ebb at present. Therefore, in various orientation and teacher training programmes, considerable importance has to be given to equip the teachers with necessary qualities and a motivation for value education.

A well-conceived programme of studies of various subjects should be provided, both in their contents and thrust. The requisite materials for value education and radical measures should be adopted to change the present degree-based, examination-oriented system with a view to unilaterally fixing the educational process on the right aims of education.

This calls for a complete overhauling of our syllabi at all levels. A content analysis of school and university curricula would reveal that the courses are hardly intended to improve the quality of the individual inasmuch as they are primarily designed for acquisition of information. So, the programme of studies should be so carefully devised as to emphasize those aspects which can readily provide to teachers and students the required opportunities, conditions and materials for value education. Secondly, specific areas of value orientation should be given special attention. Thirdly, in the totality of educational programmes, the spirit should be of value education.

Much more important than the curriculum or a particular way of instruction is the exemplary behaviour of the teacher. Even if a teacher is able to impart the highest values in the most efficient manner while in actual life he is guilty of misconduct, all his preachings will result in nothing. On the contrary, the noble character and the exemplary behaviour of a teacher will provide enough incentive to students to develop positive values of life even if such a teacher does not offer any formal instruction in value education.

While individual teachers could adopt their own strategies, an institutional plan could also be developed and implemented without much need for financial inputs or resources. The components of such an institutional plan could include the following :

(i) A critical look at the curriculum materials from the point of view of potentialities and possibilities of utilising these towards value enrichment without affecting the adopted teaching learning strategies;

(ii) Organization of co-curricular and extra-curricular activities which help in value education by observation, experience and inference. There is no need to publicise these as value inculcation efforts;

(iii) Learner and faculty interaction to appreciate and understand innovations and initiatives of voluntary efforts. Those working voluntarily for the deprived and downtrodden could also join in some of these interactions;

(iv) Utilisation of available folklore, national monuments, forms of folk-culture and indigenous expertise to imbibe a sense of belonging and pride;

(v) Critical analysis and discussion amongst the peers and with the knowledgeable could lead to appreciation of rationality and acceptance of positive impacts of science and technology.

Environment, energy, pollution, population and such other areas could be the talking points;

(vi) Utilisation of community resources and expertise through intensive interaction by making the community feel that the institution works for them and that it is functioning for improving the quality of life in general and through the instructional strategies in particular;

(vii) Providing interaction opportunities with persons of unimpeachable character, creative abilities, literary tastes, scholarly attitudes whose mere presence could motivate others;

(viii) Developing an interactive environment in the institution which nurtures response for knowledge, scholarship, learning and willingness to take responsibilities. Participatory programme like dances, dramas, debates, sports in which both the staff and the students participate could enliven the atmosphere;

(ix) Making the institutions responsive to emergent situations like floods, fire and drought. This would strengthen mutual relationship with the society; and

(x) Visits to institutions, establishements, centres of creative arts, zoos, museums and to homes for the aged and handicapped not only enhance knowledge, understanding but also generate appreciation and empathy.

Similarly the family, the peer group, the community, and, above all, the mass media could play a vital role in motivating and influencing both the teacher and the student to assimilate values and to gear themselves to value-oriented behaviour. Radio, television, newspapers, magazines and the various audio-visual aids should be utilised for value-education and character-building through formal and non-formal institutions.

6. EDUCATION FOR CHARACTER-BUILDING

It is important to note that character-building was given a prominent place in the 'gurukula' scheme of education. It was recognized by our ancient educators as the immediate aim of education. For, they observed that without character no one could utilize in life any knowledge that might have been imparted to him. Moreover, they found that even to qualify any one for acquiring knowledge of any kind, a preliminary training of the will, to a certain extent, was a necessity. Thus, the mind as the mainspring of all actions drew the devoted attention of our early educationists more than anything else. And, they have left for us a precious lore about mental training which we can ill-afford to ignore.

In the light of our ancient teaching, we should attach more importance to character-building than to the stuffing of information into our minds. Character-building, requires that pupils should be trained to feel for others, and their love should be gently led away from their little self to higher and higher spheres — family, neighbours, community, country and humanity. This will help them to be really noble in life and heroic in their deeds. Such a character-building could be achieved only through strengthening the will and chastening the heart of the student.

For strengthening the will there should be a systematic practice of concentration and self-control. Students should practise occasional fasting and silence. Furthermore, struggle against instinctive inertia for maintaining a high standard of active, methodical and well-regulated life will also contribute a good deal towards developing the will-power.

Besides strengthening the will, it is essential to give it a proper direction. And, for this, our heart has to be chastened and inspired with noble sentiments. While love for fame determines the will-path of the ordinary man of the world, love for others, community, nation and humanity directs the will of noble souls. So, we should be conscious of our environment and feel that education is meant not for the good of ourselves alone, but also for the good of humanity at large.

The first necessary thing is, we should have our faith in country and our people. We should have a proper knowledge of history and the glorious achievements of our forefathers which will certainly rouse our faith and admiration. We should see for ourselves in the museums and art galleries the characteristic beauty of Indian painting, sculpture and architecture. We should feel the grandeur of our early literature as well, especially of the magnificent epics. We need also feel proud of the contributions of ancient India to political, economic and sociological sciences. All these will awaken faith in the country and love for the people.

We should make every effort to deepen the love thus awakened by serving the people. We should participate in various nation-building activities. We should develop sympathy for the poor and downtrodden. We should understand the dignity of labour. Above all, we should realise the paramount significance of the idea, that service to the poor and needy is the real service to God.

X

EDUCATION FOR TOMORROW

1. FROM MISEDUCATION TO RE-EDUCATION

Traditional education has made stereotypes of men in their life and work situations. Historically rooted, mechanistic, authoritarian and irrelevant to life itself, the present day education may be termed mis-education. Submitting himself to the various forms of miseducation, man has lost his sense of values and the spirit of self-discovery. What is, therefore, most called for, is the adoption of a completely new system of education and training in which self-awareness, self-employment and self-achievement will be emphasized.

Concerned very much with the past, current education ignores the present and hardly bothers about the future. Content-wise its emphasis is mostly historical — always a backward emphasis on what has happened, seldom encouraging perception of what is happening and what is likely to happen.

Mechanistic in terms of the process of both teaching and learning, current education lays emphasis chiefly on memory, something a modern computer can do more effectively. There is very little concern with insight or understanding — something a computer cannot do. Discretion, reflection, intuition are all subservient to sucking and vomiting information.

Grossly authoritarian in character, current education discourages genuine enquiry. Questioning basic issues is forbidden. Its goal is regimentation instead of development of individuality. It puts the teacher under the shadow of authority and the student under the fear of the teacher.

Above all, current education has become largely irrelevant both to life and to vocation. It does not permit the discovery of personal values.

It teaches grammar, for instance, but ignores the impact of language on thought. It teaches how to solve problems in algebra, but not how to resolve conflicts in life.

A victim of the bane of the present miseducation, the adolescent prostitutes his youth, his energy and his spontaneity to either film stars or cricket heroes, or falls a prey to the cunning diplomacy of political leaders. He has no genuine questions to ask, and no sense of personal or social responsibility. He has lost contact with his true self and is in pursuit of goals that are anti-human and self-defeating. A change in the present state of affairs could be effected only by moving away from miseducation to psychological re-education.

Since current education is concerned mainly with the historical, re-education should lay greater emphasis on the here and now. If conventional education describes what has happened, re-education must deal with the perception of what is happening. The proportion of knowledge to be imparted must be about 25 per cent of the past, 50 per cent of the present and 25 per cent of the future. The more we move away from the backward emphasis the greater the opportunity for dealing creatively with the unique challenges of today.

If the conventional education is mechanistic, re-education should be dynamic and pay attention to the process of learning as discovering. It means not using the mind as a memory box. The process of teaching has to be the process of encouraging meaning-making by the learner for himself.

If current education suffocates enquiry by regimentation instead of liberating the student's mind to question what the teacher says, the re-education system does away with teachers and replaces them by catalysts who encourage discussion among students as well as between teachers and students for the emergence of spontaneous insight.

To make education extremely relevant to life and vocation, re-education must put an end to predetermined curriculum by letting learner determine what is worth learning. If conventional education starts with the teacher and curriculum, re-education must start with the student and his questions. Education then becomes a co-operative endeavour in learning instead of a unilateral enforcement of what the teacher thinks he should teach.

The philosophy behind all these corrective educational measures is simple. It means to help man to return to his own true self. No social change can take place unless it happens in the selfhood of each of us. This awakening of the selfhood should be the task of re-education. The effort to bring about social reform merely by organizational and structural changes is doomed to failure in the long run since the individual can distort or bypass the structure in thousand ways. What we have to attempt then is to initiate an educational process in which man flowers into himself.

2. TOWARDS LIFE-LONG EDUCATION

Till recently, not much significance was attached to education beyond the required formal courses for undertaking any job. The initial orientation and training received in the pre-service period in schools, colleges and other institutes was considered to be sufficient for the efficient discharge of one's duties in the remaining period of service.

But, it is now increasingly realised that the education one gets before one's employment is never complete so as to enable him to discharge his duties effectively. The report of the International Commission, appointed by UNESCO on the development of education, has suggested that "every individual must be in a position to keep learning throughout his life" and that "the idea of life-long education is the keystone of the learning society". The international report thus triggered off a world-wide interest in the importance of life-long education by proposing it as the master concept for all educational policies in the years to come both for the developed and the developing countries.

Knowledge is said to be doubling approximately every eight to ten years with the result that some of the new discoveries and inventions outpace an individual's capacity even to comprehend them. This tremendous growth in knowledge requires every one to reorient one's long established concepts and understandings, views and images, values and principles, and beliefs and convictions so that one may adjust to the demands of the new situations and be able to contribute to modern changing environments and to absorb an ever-expanding and changing body of knowledge, there is a need for some mechanism by which all workers continue their professional growth. They need to advance constantly and to be stimulated professionally through a variety of activities throughout their work tenure.

Thus, the requirements of a rapidly changing society, the continuing need for renewing professional and vocational knowledge and skills, and the desire to explore new interests and latent capacities have given a new impetus to the concept of life-long education. As J.C. Muffit puts it, "This is an age of change. It requires new and rapid adjustment. Its impact is an on-going challange. It is the basic reason determining the need for continuous education of all people."

This realization has resulted in a number of ways of keeping oneself abreast of what is happening all around. There are numerous techniques adopted for on-the-job training such as conferences, seminars, workshops, symposia and study groups and discussions. There are correspondence courses, home-study courses and courses taught overseas. Besides, there are updating courses, refresher courses, training courses, and retraining courses. These pertain to all professionals, and workers like teachers, doctors, lawyers, journalists, engineers, druggists, policemen, administrators, business magnates, foremen, industrialists and even house-wives and house-maids.

However, in a country like India, the need for the continued education of workers and professionals is likely to be felt much more in the future than at present. Increasing stress on technological advancements is likely to better the prospects for change of careers in one's life. This necessitates retraining as well as upgrading of the skills of persons in various walks of life.

Life-long education has, therefore, to be taken as the major goal for framing educational policies at different levels from the primary school to the university. The responsibility of promoting life-long education not only rests with the educational institutions but extends to many agencies — the institutions for professional training, press, magazines, radio, television and the community at large. Thus, both the formal and informal agencies of education have to rise to the occasion by making necessary changes in their policies and goals.

3. TOWARDS A BROAD-BASED, FUTURE-FOCUSED CURRICULUM

A mechanical hold-over from the past, the present curriculum in our schools and colleges is not based on any well-thought out conception of contemporary human needs. Nor is it based on any grasp of the future, on any understanding of the skills that the student will require to live in the hurricane's eye of change. The youngsters are given little choice in determining what they wish to learn. What is worse, there are hardly any variations from school to school. The future utility of what they are forced to learn is also highly questionable.

Hence, the need to update the present school curriculum with future-focused orientation. Nothing should be included in a curriculum unless it can be strongly justified in terms of relevance to the present and, what is more, meaning in the future. If this means scrapping a substantial part of formal curriculum, it must be done so. There must be a systematic way to make curricular changes without necessarily triggering intramural conflict. While it is important to preserve aspects of the present curriculum and to introduce changes gradually, we need more than haphazard attempts to modernize.

Instead of a standardized curriculum in which all students are essentially exposed to the same subjects, an attempt should be made to create a widely diversified range of disciplines. Students should be permitted far greater choice than at present, keeping in mind future needs. Also, they should be encouraged to taste a wide variety of short-term courses before making long-term commitments.

The range of subject-matter should be broad enough so that some provision could be made for dealing with the unknown, the unexpected and the possible apart from dealing with the 'known' elements. The children should be introduced to the wonders of outer space as well as to the submarines. By moving in this direction and creating contingency curricula, the society can bank a wide range of skills that will be of immense use to meet the challenges of the future.

The students should also be grounded in certain common skills needed for human communication and social integration. Schools must teach not merely data, but ways to manipulate it. They must learn how to discord old ideas, how and when to replace them. By instructing students how to learn, unlearn and relearn, a powerful new dimension can be added to education. As a psychologist explains, "The new education must teach the individual how to classify and reclassify information, how to evaluate its veracity, how to change categories when necessary, how to move from the concrete to the abstract and back, how to look at problems from a new direction — how to teach himself."

Education concerns itself as much with the inculcation of moral values as with the transmission of skills. In the present curriculum students are seldom made to analyze their own values. Thus, millions are passing through the education system without having been forced to search out the contradictions in their own value systems, to probe their own life goals deeply, or even to discuss these matters candidly with their teachers and peers. Instead of imposing a rigid set of values as at present the curriculum must include formal and informal activities that help the student define, explicate and test his values.

To sum up, the present curriculum must be so modified as to include not only a wide range of data-oriented courses, but also elements of the unknown, common skills, moral values and a strong emphasis on relevance and meaning in terms of the present and future. In other words, the curriculum must combine a great variety of factual content with universal training in what might be termed 'life know-how'.

4. FROM A GRIM TODAY TO A GRAND TOMORROW

Most of our creative energy and financial resources have all along been directed to technical rather than to human innovation. We seem to be more concerned with making better things than better people. The question that we may pursue is not how we can produce more, faster and at less cost, but how we can learn more about human nature and talents, so that technology becomes man's servant and not his master. The time has now come to discover and apply the inner human resources in order to explore what is and to create what has never been.

Modern psychology reveals that man has hitherto unsuspected and untapped resources of a versatile kind. Many potentialities of human nature have been identified by psychologists. Some of them are extra sensory perception (ESP), achievement motive and creativity. Creativity as a significant mode of intellectual potentiality has recently been identified by Prof. J.P. Guilford. Creativity is concerned with divergent ways of finding solutions to the problems as opposed to seeking one 'correct' answer through what is termed a convergent mode of thinking.

Today, we need men given not only to good judgement, but also to originality and creativity. We need men who not only solve problems but find problems ahead of time. Problems exist because we have not thought of them before. So, what we need is anticipatory thinking. We do have men of creative abilities who possess distinct motivational characteristics. They have to be identified and properly encouraged. As Arnold Toynbee has rightly pointed out, "To give a fair chance to potential creativity is a matter of life and death for any society .... because the outstanding creative ability of a fairly small percentage of the population is mankind's ultimate capital asset."

Efforts to motivate, train or develop human potentialities require great ingenuity. No ready-made technique is available for realization of potentialities, especially in the case of creative potentiality. The best course under the present circumstances is to create an awareness in the individuals of their talents. Not only an individual has, within himself, vast resources, but he has resources for self-understanding. Providing opportunities for a wide variety of experiences and a climate of facilitative psychological attitudes, and involving the personnel in planning the development of the organization will go a long way in providing 'catalytic effect' on the creative individual.

Awareness of one's potentialities can be created through a number of psychological techniques such as T-group training, Sensitivity Training, Brain Storming Technique, Bionics, Synectics, Transactional Analysis (TA). These techniques help to free creative expression from conscious and unconscious inhibitions. Furthermore, group dynamics, involving heterogeneous members, might facilitate a congenial atmosphere for the bringing out of hidden talents and latent potentialities.

To develop human resources and faculties, emphasis should also be laid on power motivation and extension motivation. Power motivation helps a person to use his influence in developing competence and power over other people. Extension motivation is reflected in the concern one has for other human beings, and for the society and group of which he is a member. Such psychological re-education to emphasize extension motivation through motivation development programmes, using feedback as the basic approach, can be very effective in the transition of our society from a grim today to a grand tomorrow.

5. EDUCATION FOR TOMORROW

Today, every pupil, in virtually every school, is required to study history. He studies history. He studies ancient Greece and Rome, the rise of feudalism, the fall of Moghal empire, the British rule, the Independence movement in India, and so on and so forth. He is introduced to patriotic legends, and is peppered with endless accounts of wars, revolutions and upheavals. Thus, the present day student is steeped, to the extent possible, in his nation's past and that of the world.

The student is also introduced, at some point or other, to current events. Important news items of the day are written on the school common board for information of students. And some enterprising class teachers ask their students to bring in newspaper clippings. Thus, the modern student is offered a thin salver of the present too.

But, surprisingly enough, the school is silent about tomorrow. There is no provision whatsoever in the curriculum for analysing and evaluating future possibilities and probabilities. Rooted in the past, the curriculum is not based on any grasp of the future, any understanding of the skills the student will require to face the challenges of the future confidently and successfully. It looks as through the future was banned from the classroom as well as from the student's consciousness. Thus, the student is focused backward instead of forward.

But, it is no longer sufficient for the present day student to understand the past. It is not even enough for him to understand the present. He must learn to anticipate the directions and rate of change. He must learn to make repeated probabilistic, increasingly long-range assumptions about the future. If our children are to adapt more successfully to rapid change, we must sensitize them to the possibilities and probabilities of tomorrow. And, we can help them adapt better if we simply provide them with advance information about what lies ahead.

There are ways to send the human mind arching forward. First of all, we must create a stronger future-consciousness on the part of the public. What is needed now is a concentrated focus on the social and personal implications of the future. We need to propagate dynamic, non-supernatural images of what temporal life will be like, what it will sound and smell and taste and feel like in the fast-onrushing future. We must also encourage people, from childhood on, to speculate freely, even fancifully, what the next generation holds in store for the entire human race.

Just as we offer our young students courses in history we should also offer courses in 'Future' — courses in which the possibilities and probabilities of the future are systematically explored. As Robert Jungk, one of Europe's leading futurist-philosophers, says, "Nowadays almost exclusive stress is laid on learning what has happened and has been done. Tomorrow .... at least one-third of all lectures and exercises ought to be concerned with scientific, technical, artistic and philosophical work in progress, anticipated crises and possible future answers to these challenges."

It is believed that we do not have a literature of the future for use in these courses. Nevertheless, we do have literature about the future, consisting not only of the great utopias but also of comtemporary science fiction which has immense value as a mind-stretching force for the creation of the habit of anticipation. Rightly studied, science fiction can lead young minds through an imaginative exploration of political, social, psychological and ethical issues that will confront the children when they become adults.

Furthermore, to sharpen the individual's future-focused role image, young students could be asked to write their own future autobiographies. If adults at eighteen are given the future biographies they themselves wrote at the age of twelve, they can see how maturation has altered their own images of the future. Thus, this technique can be used to help the student understand how his values, talents, skills and knowledge have shaped his own possibilities. Linked with the study of probability and simple methods of prediction, such exercises can delineate and modify each individual's conception of the future. They can also create a new individual time-bias, a new sensitivity to tomorrow that will prove helpful in coping with the exigencies of the present.

On top of that, 'Councils of the Future' consisting of teams of men and women devoted to probing the future could be created in every school and college. By projecting 'assumed futures', and by defining coherent educational responses to them, such councils could have a powerful impact on education.

INDEX

N

O

P

R

S

T

U

Atlantic
APP
9030
13/6/02